SPIRIT TEACHINGS FROM THE HIGHEST SOURCE

(Spiritual Meditations)

Written by Spirit and Transcribed by
Brendan O'Callaghan

I.S.M. Publications

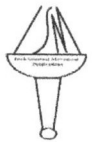

Copyright © 2021 Brendan O'Callaghan All rights reserved

The characters and events portrayed in this book are fictitious. Any similarity to real persons, living or dead, is coincidental and not intended by the author.

No part of this book may be reproduced, or stored in a retrieval system, or transmitted in any form or by any means, electronic, mechanical, photocopying, recording, or otherwise, without express written permission of the publisher.

ISBN: 9798700545631

Cover design by: Brendan O'Callaghan

This book is dedicated to those who have the audacity to search for the true meaning for their life on Earth, to search for their Spirit within, and who have the courage to embrace their findings. We hope that these writings might help trigger some questions and your search will provide the answers.

"The greatest fear is ignorance.

The greatest gift is the release from fear.

Wisdom is that gift.

Reject and remain fearfully ignorant.

Accept and become truly free."

'Spirit'

CONTENTS

Nothing taken for granted.	13
Is enough, enough?	17
Self-worth	21
Revolution	25
Divine order.	29
The Communicator.	33
Status in the World of Spirit.	37
The Composition of Humankind	41
Truth (1).	45
Spiritual Growth	49
Hindsight	53
Foresight.	57
Mid-summer	61
New Age Movement	65

CONTENTS contd.

Advancement	69
Truth (2).	73
The Control of Negativity	77
Hope (1).	81
Miracles	85
Making Progress	89
About Death	93
Animals and Death	97
Dying – a painless process	101
The Spirit World	105
Living	109
Control by limitation	113
Reincarnation	117
Jesus.	121
Psychological barriers	125
More on Jesus	129

CONTENTS contd.

The New Phase.	133
Religion	137
Misconceptions	141
Blind Faith	145
Belief and Truth	149
Needs and Wants (1).	153
The Centre	155
Trust in Spirit	157
Self-Examination	161
Testing times	165
Greater teachings	169
The Spiral of Greed	173
The Epitome of misfortune	177
Crime and Punishment	181
Orthodox Religions	185
Spiritual Development (1).	189
Spiritual Development (2)	193

CONTENTS contd.

Spiritual Development (3).	197
New Philosophy	201
Words for a winter solstice	205
Prayer	209
Needs and wants (2).	213
Ego and Humility	217
Power	221
Resolutions	225
Reflections.	227
Badness	231
The Spirit life	235
Sin (1).	239
Sin (2).	243
Earth Life	245
Human nature and the Spirit world.	249
Spirit Migration	237
Words to a Psychic	261

CONTENTS contd.

More on Spirit evolvement	265
Communication	269
Compromise	273
Death	277
Perfect for the Job	281
Search for the Self	285
Time	289
Rationalisation	293
The Fantasy Land	297
Hope (2).	303
The Anti-Christ	307
Multidimensional Knowledge	311
Journey into the Spirit World	315
Trance	319

INTRODUCTION.

These are a set of channelled writings; some might call them meditations. At the time I received them I was experiencing health difficulties and was not able to personally attend the meditation evenings in the Irish Spiritual Centre, in Dublin. In my absence, and in order to help the facilitators in the meditation groups there, Spirit gave me these teachings. I was able to electronically transfer them into the Centre.

At the request of Spirit, and the requests of many who have enjoyed these teachings I have now put them into book format. These writings make good reading for any meditation group, or for any individual who is earnestly seeking to return to their true spirituality and resume their spiritual path.

I hope you will find them instructive and that they can guide you through the morass of disinformation and misinformation that is being expounded under the heading of spirituality. It would be good if initially you did not apply intellectual analysis to these words as you go along. Read each chapter first, meditate on it and then see your truth from the awareness gained. Spirit will always be there for you and your personal Spirit Guide, Guardian Angel, Friend from the Light, will be able to nudge you in the direction you need to take in your personal quest, a duty no other can honestly do for you.

I thank you on behalf of Spirit for giving your Spirit the use of your being to further the work of The Spirit, the work of God. We thank you for taking the time to read these words. A happy life awaits.

NOTHING TAKEN FOR GRANTED.

Fortune rarely blesses the fortunate. This statement will, we feel, provoke some thought. We need to understand the meaning of fortune and fortunate. They are unrelated words. We could say that it is fortunate that fortune never favours the fortunate. Now this statement is starting to become understandable. In the normal sense of the word, fortune indicates that somebody who receives or inherits one would become financially better off. Better off, that's another statement we will have to examine later. To be fortunate is to have something wonderful happen for or to you – an event that was unexpected by oneself even if obvious to others. So, we can see that there is a difference between these words. A fortunate event need not carry fortune with it to make it worthy of the description fortunate.

Of all the fortunate events that you have experienced how many of them have involved fortune? Maybe none! Yet they have been very fortunate and very often no amount of financial benefit could have given you what it was that you received through your good fortune.

We need to look away from the financial measure of wealth. We miss so much because we cannot put a price on it. If you were to receive a gift of little or no financial value where do you display it? It might carry a spiritual value beyond anything that money can buy yet it will take second or less place next to the gold clock. Take the contents of your handbag, brief case or pocket, what is it that you most value in it. Is it your bankcard? Your battered, torn photograph of Granny that the negatives of which are long lost. I suspect that it will be the photograph. The loss of this photograph will be regretted for the rest of your days. When you tell your grandchildren about your Granny wouldn't it be nice if you could have a photograph to show them and for you to remember her by? We have forgotten already about the loss of the bankcard. Therefore, let us not concern ourselves with the attainment of fortune. Fortune follows the fortunate.

We always acknowledge the happiness of others no matter what their plight may appear to be. We can see that people can live a happy and full life under what appears to be deplorable conditions. We see that they are happy and yet we seek to place our miserable lives as the example they should follow. We teach them our values, our dependency and bring into their lives all the tools that will ensure that they come under our influence and therefore control. Do you find this hard to understand or accept? Look at our children. How much advertising is aimed at them? You should have this or that toy. What do we do? We join in on this control adding that we will help the child gain this toy- provided the child behaves itself – the way we want it to. The manipulation of the child's value has begun and indeed the controlled unnatural behaviour begins to take the place of the child's own chosen personality. What do I mean by "chosen personality"? Remember that it is Spirit that has designed this world for it to evolve through. It is the Spirit that individually automates the particular body that it has chosen to incarnate into. This has been a spiritual decision for spiritual reason therefore the chosen body needs to have particular individual traits or personality that would be required by the Spirit in order for that Spirit receive the benefit of this particular incarnation. If we change or influence that personality, we are doing a great disservice to the incarnate Spirit. We can see in the history of mankind how we have "educated the savages" to their detriment. Look into the vegetable plot. No longer are we content to grow indigenous vegetables. We grow potatoes, peppers and all sorts of difficult and inappropriate food in order that we can show our superiority over our neighbour. How will we feel when our crop fails and we look into our neighbour's garden full of the necessities to sustain life?

Fortune rarely blesses the fortunate. We can look at this statement again. In the way that we measure its value we can again question why it doesn't. Isn't it fortunate that the sun rises every day? Isn't it fortunate that we are still alive in the morning? If you agree with these statements, you will agree that it is indeed good fortune that God is so beneficent so as to supply us with these essentials; that it is good fortune that God has created this wonderful universe to evolve through; that is even greater fortune to know that all this is so that we can take our rightful place within the Godhead. God Blesses you all

IS ENOUGH, ENOUGH?

Accumulation is a funny word. We need to examine its function in our vocabulary. This word tells us that we gather things together and store them indefinitely. We often suggest Human beings must be related to the squirrel. This is an insult to that wonderful animal. Human beings might have similar habits to the squirrel but we could find a better way of employing these habits. The squirrel gathers what it needs for its nourishment and survival. The magpie also is a gatherer/accumulator. The magpie is attracted to thing bright to adorn its nest. The squirrel eats its accumulated nuts and the magpie discards its hoard of shiny things once the need for the nest has passed. The human animal however accumulates and hoards anything often indefinitely. Have you ever cleared out the belongings of someone who has departed this physical world? We often find it strange that there is so much that had been stored and appeared to have no value that we can see. The most important things in life are readily available to us. God in his creation gave us an inheritance that has no equal. God didn't give us what we mostly hoard e.g. money and other material goods. Mankind concentrates his mind on gaining the un-necessities of life. Man becomes subservient to these un-necessities. These un-necessities are addictive and in their lacking of goodness can never satisfy the hunger that we develop around them. Now think of the hours in every day we spend seeking the means to feed this accumulative habit. We become preoccupied in life by directing our thoughts into the procuring of things in life. Why do we go to work or feel the need to work? Isn't it so that we can earn the money to buy goods with, whether those goods be a house, food, or even a car? Think of why we need to have an automatic washing machine – it is so that we can put our soiled cloths into it and leave the machine to do the work. We don't have the time anymore to do the washing. We can even employ other people to do other work for us – because we don't have the time to do it ourselves. You might claim that you haven't the skill – all skills can be learnt if we give the time to it. You can employ another to do a job for you, that you are skilled enough to do, but your earning capacity is greater than theirs – if you are to do your job, you will earn sufficient to pay the tradesman and still have profit to indulge yourself in your accumulating habits. If you have the time you might even think of others things you wish to add to your list of "accumulatables".

If we can change our thinking to achieve sufficiency rather than insufficiency, we can begin to put our life time into order. If you knew where your next meal was coming from you would not preoccupy yourself with those thoughts of accumulating enough food around you to ensure you will at least have enough for your next meal – and perhaps the one after it. The marketing strategy of most food providers is telling us that the least we can buy is a packet of goods. Now this packet might contain twice as much as we need but it is better to be safe than sorry. We can keep the rest for another day. We are being trained to accumulate but not what we want (remember we couldn't buy a half packet) but what the marketing organisations want us to.

How many items in your weekly shopping are excess quantities? How much of the items in your food cupboard are stored because you wanted to store them? How many items were forced upon you through "good" marketing strategy? Try buying legal measures of motor fuel. You cannot. You can only buy more or less. More will ensure you will get home with some to spare whereas less will ensure you won't have enough to get home at all. What is the greatest fear of a smoker? They fear they will not have a cigarette when they need one and usually, they will have to carry an excessive number of cigarettes to ensure they will not be short. The list can go on and on. It is for us to be aware of the tendency to be an accumulator irrespective of the excuses we might afford ourselves. It is after all ourselves who will suffer in the long run. We will have no accommodation, be it in space or time for all the good things in life, all the God things in life.

Go in peace and rest in the Love of God the Supreme creator of all things good and bad.

SELF-WORTH.

We have been speaking about worth. We talked about the value of fortune and we talked about the value of accumulation. How much do you value yourself? This is a very important question that deserves to be pondered upon and perhaps never answered. There is only one person who can realise your value and that is yourself.

Nobody is as unique as you are – to you. Everybody is unique in that there is no other who has everything that you have. For example, (1) there are possibly others who have a similar genetic make-up as you – your brothers and sisters. But are they the same sex as you? If they are, are they older or younger than you are? Were there any events in your parent's life between the conceptions that might have affected their health and thus eliminated or added to the gene pool. Remember that in this world nothing can avoid perpetual change even though we might try. So this is one way that would suggest that you are unique, even different to your brothers and sisters. (2) There is also the influence of your place, date and time of birth. This applies also to twins. Even a short space of times between births can make a difference. Astrology illustrates this very precisely. We know that the winter sun in Ireland doesn't give a suntan. The reason for this is that the angle of the sun and thus its intensity is not as powerful as the summer sun. In winter in order to get a suntan we have to change our geographical location to where the intensity of the sun is greater. All things in this world of ours are subjected to the influences of the planets in some way. Different planets affect the individuals differently according to their personal horoscope. So, this affects personality and behaviour and the ability to handle life events as we encounter them. (3) Nobody can see life through your eyes. Therefore your "outlook" on life is entirely personal. We could go on with these examples. It may be a good exercise for you to discover is how different you are to everybody you know. The differences are illustrations of your uniqueness.

These differences are also indicators to your self-worth. We hear expressions such as two heads are better than one. Did you ever stop to consider why? Perhaps it is that the second head adds its own unique experience to the collective, an added dimension. Have you ever looked at the world around you with one eye? It appears quite different than with two eyes. Try looking at the world with one eye and then the other and you will see that the two views are so different. The artist who shares their vision with us shows us a way of looking at things that we were unaware of. The pleasure of this artists sharing is a measure of their worth in the art world.

When you begin to see your uniqueness, you begin to see the value that you have to share with the world. After your meditation when you share your journey with your fellow travellers you will often trigger an understanding of their own personal journey for them because you have added your view, your dimension to the overall picture. You have added your uniqueness. To-night instead of perhaps being impatient as a fellow sitter laboriously goes through their experience, add this experience to yours for the above reason. You are then recognising their worth in the group.

If we can be conscious of our worth and the worth of those around us, we can lead a much fuller life. If we can concentrate on discovering our own unique worth, we can then begin to apply this to our living. The nice thing about our worth is that we are born with it. Why then is it so hard to discover? Maybe the answer is that we listen to others telling us how we should be. This personality they are seeking to change us into invariably is to allow themselves to be other than who they are. If we change to suit them then we do them and ourselves a great disservice. Be who you are. You are who you were divinely inspired to be long before you were born. Go with God's blessing proud and happy to be who you are with a strong sense of your unique worth to the world.

REVOLUTION.

I hope you have managed to keep your mind open about what has been said to date. It would be good if you found some conflict with your feeling regarding what has been said. To sit back in subservience has been a habit that mankind has developed to its detriment. Argue, contradict, be sceptical, be challenged and be challenging. These are all qualities. Blind faith must not be allowed to continue. For too long mankind has accepted that he must bend to the will of the emperor. This age will see an end to that meekness. You have been told that the meek shall inherit the earth. You have not been told that the meek will still be servants to the masters who would not stoop so low to toil in the earth.

We have stressed to you it is important that you discover who you are and find a great value in that. You chose to be born into this revolutionary age and there you will also find a need to revolt. We do not talk of bloody conflict rather a development of an infallible philosophy that is pertinent to you. In this way you can continue your way along your path in confidence that you know the way and do not need to be led. You will find that this way of life will automatically take you on the happy path – right into the lap of God. Self-power, self-knowing are the abilities that you will gain along the way. Recognise that in your everyday life the everyday things distract you. You walk down the street, and in the process, expose yourself to all types of temptations. That object in the shop window that has been strategically placed and polished so as to take from a similar object you already have. There is nothing wrong with the one you have except it doesn't have all the features that the current model has and also it has lost its gloss. Yet you feel that you must put yourself into a subservient position in order to procure the one in the window. You are offered a ridiculous price for the one you have – simply because it is not as new and shiny as the one you wish to purchase and of course it is not this year's model. You are not told that it is less reliable than the original and that the guarantee is not as effective as the one originally given. You borrow beyond your means. (Any borrowing is beyond your means – the means available to you couldn't afford it and that is why you needed to borrow). The new object fails to live up to its 'super dooper' image and now you have two things you didn't need and no means (to get out of your difficulty).

What about the fellow traveller who suggests that their way is the best and only way for you to go? Only one person can stand in the same place at the same time. Do you go before them? Do you go behind them? Do you go beside them? If you go before them are you the guinea pig? If you go behind them are you being led? If you walk beside them you will find that you need to keep in step and they are setting the pace. You will notice that Spirit never leads, never pushes but guides you through the development of the sensitivity that your natural chosen being possesses.

Never surrender yourself to God. You might find this a strange suggestion. To surrender yourself to God you are in effect handing over the responsibility that you came unto this earth to use as a tool to your evolvement. If God were to accept your offer God would be inhibiting your development. This situation lacks any benefit to God or mankind. Remember that all you need you have. What you seek is the understanding of the immense power that you have. You see God as being all powerful. You are a part of God and therefore in that part share this all-powerfulness. This is why evolution has to be so exact. If you do not know the power you possess how can God in his goodness permit you to access that power. We have outlined some of the obvious indications that you are as yet unready to share in this power. All mankind has still much learning to do. This is not a reflection on the ignorance of mankind rather an indication of how far mankind has already come and still has to go. We hope this writing will help you i your task. Go with God's love illuminating your heart, providing you with the light to see the map of your journey.

God blesses you all.

DIVINE ORDER.

My friends I feel from you that the words already delivered to you have touched something within you. It is not expected that you will fully understand the importance of these initial moves but be assured that movement there is. We thank you for your tolerance. It can be appreciated that the information we wish to impart to you does not come within the abilities of any earth known language to communicate. This is why we continuously open the doors of your mind, causing you to question more. The only way to get an answer is to ask a question. The question you need to ask is also confined by the inadequacies of your language and therefore often remains unasked and consequently unanswered. By opening the doorway in your mind, you can indeed address the question and also in return through the same portal receive the Divine answer – often in the form of a knowing that cannot be verbalised in your tongue. This is why we communicate as we do. It may not fit into any pattern that you are familiar with but your familiar patterns are not, and cannot, provide the answer that is needed. This is why you often feel dissatisfied with the world in which you live, or should we say struggle. Therefore, if we were to repeat these same patterns you would end up as confused as ever.

Have you ever wondered if there is any such thing as Divine order? There is and one of the problems that mankind encounters is mans need to reorder. Why is it that man cannot leave the order in place and work with it instead of thinking that it is a duty to disrupt and improve that which is already perfect? These are some of the questions that must be confronted before any real advantageous change can take place. The Divine plan is perfect, conceived by the epitome of perfection, God. It is not a dull un-developing plan. God is motion. God is emotion. God is LOVE. How ignorant to think that God would develop the universe for a specified time without allowing for progress towards that end. We know that nothing is stationary totally. Even as you lie in your bed asleep you might think that you are in a stationary position. You are not. You are getting older. Your mind is active and your body is in a state of repair for your next day. You might say that death provides for a stationary state but the Spirit has removed itself from the body to continue on its path, and the body has set itself the task of self-disposal. There is at no stage the opportunity of being stationary. The planet earth is constantly revolving and as long as you are on that plant you have to go around with it.

It is necessary to discover, on the hypothesis that this is a perfect situation, how you can work in with this wonderful plan. We would like to give you some simple advice. Get as still as you can, allowing for all that has been said. You have an expression "go with the flow". That will do for a start. Don't just go with the flow, use the time and space to allow yourself to observe the plan, to discover the plan. The start of this is simple. You are aware that day invariably follows night? So, you begin to observe the Divine plan in action. Isn't that simple? You might think simplistic? If you think it simplistic then you are only showing your ignorance. You are looking at fact and seeing the marvel of God's creation in its simplest and most obvious form. You only had to observe. We could give you so many examples and many of these examples you would initially dispute. The truth never goes away. It is always there no matter how much you may dispute it. Your thinking is constantly changing in relation to truth. Stand and observe the truth without dispute, once you learn how to do it, and you will save yourself a lot of experiences that can only come through confrontation – with your own ignorance.

We will go now and let your mind repair! Know constantly that you are a wonderful and important part of the Divine plan and heaven would not be the same without you.

We go. God Blesses you all. We love you through the power of God.

THE COMMUNICATOR.

You have been reading my words for these past weeks and as yet I have not introduced who I am. This is not rudeness - rather timing. It has always been my intention to introduce you to the amazing, (by your terms), technology, (by our terms), of Spirit communication. This can be best achieved by my introducing myself.

I am who I am in that I am a composition of many facets that comprise the source of knowledge. In the world of Spirit, we are all one. In your world you are all one though you usually fail to recognise this. It is when you deliberately cease trying to be one that you experience trouble, whether it is in your health or more obviously in your happiness. You go against the laws of nature – your nature and God – and look instead for your individuality. This is where you begin to experience the difficulties with what is called ego. To belong to one removes this problem and allows the better flow of harmony to exist. But more on this later. The oneness of Spirit allows us, the individual Spirit, to find the special qualities we individually have and then to express them as a team. Everybody (this is how Spirit terms the collective incarnate beings) has much in common but it is what they don't have in common that makes them individual. If you, like us, could find this individuality a bonding tool with your fellow beings you would go a long way to progressing towards Spirit. You will see then that what we have already told you begins to fit more into the picture that we seek to demonstrate to you. These communications illustrate how this teamwork can be effective.

I am "that", which is known to Brendan as the Essence. The reason for this title is because my composition is of many parts of many Spirit beings that have contributed their individuality to form this source, that is now being used with the co-operation of Brendan, to deliver these messages to you. It is through that essence of individuality of Brendan that the channel between our worlds is completed. Brendan has bonded with us here in Spirit through his individuality. He is part of the team and also a part of the Essence – me.

Then you know me if you know Brendan and if you know me then you too by a decision, through the knowledge and free will that is yours, can also bond with Spirit and therefore with God. You are aware that Brendan exists and obviously these words are not his and therefore we exist, you will thus understand that you do not have to wait until death to make the bond with God.

We spoke earlier that life – earthly life, is for living to its best and most fulfilling end. This does not imply that gay abandon is the way to live it either. Remember that the best way to discover fulfilment is to find what it is you enjoy. We see enjoyment as being a celebration of God. How often do you discover that it is the simple things of life that are the most satisfying? We often hear you people exclaim the relief you feel when a festive occasion comes to an end and you can return to normal. You return to the normal simple things of life – without the excesses that you seem to require in order to celebrate

We do not wish to criticise any individual's way of life, but we do say if you feel that this applies to you then we have drawn you into an awareness that you might act upon. There is another myth that we would like to dispel. There is no judgmental God waiting to sort out the just from the unjust. It is not necessary that God undertake this task. You will have already done the judging of yourself. We illustrate this with the first sections of this paragraph. Do you find that we criticise you? We don't, but you feel the "guilt" around the awareness and thus punish yourself. Remember if you understand the necessity that took you on the course of action that you feel we criticise you for, and take full responsibility for your actions and outcome, then you will have learnt a valuable lesson in what it is, in this particular exercise, that is preventing you from the bonding we spoke of earlier.

Go ponder these words for now. Learn to understand your individual motivation and you will see that indeed you are preparing a perfect surface for the coming together of us all.

Go in God's Light, with God's Love and blessing.

STATUS IN THE WORLD OF SPIRIT.

Friends, there are many misnomers we would like to address at this point. When last we wrote we spoke of attaining or re-attaining the oneness with the One and still possess an awareness of the individuality that enhances the facilities of the Oneness. We also addressed an understanding of Spirit, the essence of all living things. It was suggested that to isolate the individuality from the oneness was a dangerous act as was isolating the oneness from the individuality.

When Angels are spoken of they tend to be individualised, to have special attributes. Michael is considered to be the archangel but this is indeed a dangerous practice if it is not understood properly. Mankind has created a hierarchy of Angels giving them names and title. Mankind has constantly done this to the detriment of the good works that could emanate from that essence. If a name is given to anything that then becomes a term of recognition. When a title is added to that name that name achieves a status. In Spirit there is no status. How can there be when it is a Oneness? The other damaging factor of this title is that sides can be drawn, e.g. "My Angel is better than yours", etc. While mankind bickers about who is greater or better than another, progress stands still. Look into your history and the wars that have and are being fought over who's Deity is the one true one and you'll see what we mean.

There are no Angels only Spirits. All Spirits are part of the Oneness. You may call them whatever name you wish be it Angel or Spirit or Friend. We prefer Friend. You will hear people talking about Angels but know they are not on the friendly terms we speak of. If you could see the disturbance caused to Spirit by these petty power games the man plays on man.

We would next like to talk about Fairies. They do exist. They have title and they have status. They are not very evolved in that they are engrossed in nature and do not understand the Divinity of nature. To them all is as it is. They possess senses like a mortal being and this is what keeps them as they are. They are trapped. They are neither good nor bad. Remember to them everything is as it is. If you disturb them, they react very much as a human or indeed any other animal would react. Frighten them and they will frighten you back. Respect them and they will respect you back. Ask them for help and they will help but again like the human animal will expect something in return. They are very much part of the world and must be allowed to live out that part. They eventually do evolve into a greater understanding. Everything in your world is at some stage in its evolution. In that state it is perfect and must never be deemed to be greater or lesser than anything else.

It is difficult for you to understand a non-status existence. You are being continuously educated into becoming greater than the next person. You are encouraged to reach the top of the class, to reach the top of your career, to have the biggest and best of everything. The controllers of the world will encourage you to this "excellence" and willingly help you into servitude to the controllers for the rest of your earthly life. These controllers can be embodied or disembodied. No other animal controls another into servitude except perhaps the ant and then only certain species of them. Mankind looks to the other animals and insects to see how "intelligent" they are. If it is seen that they are engaged in some routine that is similar to the behaviour of Man they are seen as expressing certain intelligence. Most of the practices of Mankind are not intelligent when viewed from an evolving perspective. Mankind perpetuates ignorance and stalls the evolving process. Mankind stifles true growth and turns it to Mans own end. If Man is not enlightened how can this growth be seen to be continuing in an evolving process when it is controlled by un-enlightened beings?

Man needs to see things as they are, constantly expanding and maintaining just one step ahead of Mans development. If Man keeps seeking, Man will constantly develop one step behind Spirit.

That is enough for now. Go rest in the Heart of God, snuggle into His Love, and receive His Blessed Kiss.

THE COMPOSITION OF HUMANKIND.

More myths need exploring. In order for the truth to be discovered it is necessary to take away the untruths. It has been said that the best lie is the truth mis-told. This then is our reason for this communication. When Mankind sets out to enhance its egotistical position it must first remove the obstacles to achieving what it perceives to be Mankind just position. The Laws of Spirit would always be true and should be above the need to interpret. Mankind needs to re-interpret these Laws in order that they do not impede Mankind's dishonest growth. These words might at first appear to accuse Mankind of manipulating the Laws of God. We see this as Mankind being dictated to by his own ego. Egotistical people see themselves as being uncontrolled by external powers and therefore this self-righteous opinion leaves them subject to the negative aspects of themselves.

Mankind is a composition of body, mind and Spirit. We would like you to consider the mind as being a state of awareness. If the mind is a state of awareness then the degree of awareness of that mind indicates the stage that being has achieved in its evolutionary process. Mankind therefore is body, awareness and Spirit. By Mankind following the dictates of its awareness Mankind is being controlled by a mind that is limited by its own level of development. If that awareness has only achieved the awareness of the ego then there is a strong possibility that that mind will lose itself to egotistical pursuits. Unfortunately, this is the stage most of Mankind is experiencing. When we spoke of non-status existence, we are aware that this concept is difficult to understand unless there is an understanding of the egotistical state. Being an incarnate being the ego is a necessary part. Most of the feelings you experience are measured through using the ego. Let us say that somebody has created a situation that will affect you, (through your feelings). The degree to which that situation will affect you will depend on your ego status. If you are deeply imbedded in your ego then the feeling of hurt will be deep and the resentment for being hurt will be greater. If you are not imbedded in your ego there will be little or no hurt and consequently no resentment. The ability to continue to develop as a Spiritual human being is best served by having an ego as a part of the self, as part of your oneness and not as your controller.

The myth here is, that it is needed by Spirit that you develop yourselves into this super being with all these special powers of clairvoyance and healing etc. This is of course not true. You need to discover the wonderful being you already are and to harmonise with that self in a Spiritually incarnate way. Unfortunately, there are people in your world who seek to exploit you through the weak link that is your ego. To live your life in a status ridden way subjects to this foul misdirection. If you have special powers you must be somebody and the principle that confers these powers on you becomes your master. There is only one master and that is God. As you are part of God you are also your own master. There are some who seek the title from you.

Leave them as they are directing you for their own ends. Nobody can make you what you already are and thus if you are already empowered with the potential to be a healer then you are already a healer. All you need is the guidance in understanding what you already have and how to do your part in the directing of the power of Love.

There are those who go to religion for Spiritual reasons. There are those who go to Spirit for psychic reasons. Both are misled. Spiritual is to do with Spirit. Religion is to follow the man created divinity of some wonderful incarnation that offered guidance into Spirituality. This latter is elevated by man into a figurehead that must be religiously followed for the benefit of the prime manipulators who ruled that the incarnate was indeed a deity. This is invariably the case in religions and you will remember where we said that status could be used to create divisions and wars. Psychic searching is often a search for status and power. There is no difference between psychosis and psychic. You will see that many who seek the psychic do indeed loose themselves into the ego and eventually, (unless some encounter redirects them), become what is termed psychotic. We say psychic is Spirit without direction.

Do not let these words disturb you. Those who find these words as an affront need to read them again and to ensure that they are not the victims of the myth that they must achieve the status of master. There is no such title in Spirit.

Go with God's Love and face into the world a stronger and wiser Spirit armed with these loving words.

TRUTH (1).

You may be surprised at our attitude towards you this week. We realise that we have been very strict with you. This is not to avoid the necessity that we felt to apply this strictness. The truth is true no-matter how it is applied. What is extremely important to realise is that mankind has got lazy in accepting the truth and thus when he is called to recognise it he finds it hard to accept that he has strayed so far from it. Man's first instinct when confronted is to attack the one confronting. This is the first line of defence. We find it quite common that man will defend his ignorance by attacking the truth. However, we come in love and understanding. What we impart to you is the universal truth as produced through the perfection of creation. We cannot vary this in any way no-matter how difficult it might seem.

We come in the name of God. We are from the Light. We teach the truth no-matter how difficult it is. There can be no compromise for the truth. You will no doubt have experienced the truth haunting you until it is allowed to manifest. You are wonderful beings even if you find that your spiritual growth is difficult. Never feel that you test our patience, as we do not have such a condition. We are in a state of timelessness and therefore have all the time we need. You too have all the time you need but your world is constantly stressing the shortness of that commodity and thus able to put you under a form of fear and control. You understand what it is we are saying. If you had all the time you needed there would be no pressure upon you. "The only pressure is time, where there is no time there is no pressure". What do you see as you rush to work, or indeed as you rush? Usually nothing. If you had the time to look it would all appear different. Do you like rising early in the morning? If you don't why don't you, and if you do, why do you? Ask your friends and compare what they say to what you say. It will be interesting to see the results. You miss a lot of life and truth by languishing in that semi-sleep state. You get trapped in a pattern again. We have talked of patterns before. Instead of training yourself into living an "normal" life try discovering what your own personal life shows you and train yourself to live that.

You will find that there are those who would like you to emulate them by following their habits. If it is that they have devised a unique way of living that seems to make them happy and well then, they may indeed have found their way to live their life to the full. But it is their way. You may test some of their ways on yourself, testing so that you will see how appropriate it is for you. There is no universal, finite way of life other than the truth. The truth is dynamic and personal. Your truth is specific to you. When we say we teach the truth you will notice that we present challenges to you so you may discover how you truly feel. Careful analysis on your part will help you identify your truth. You will find that you can then live by that truth and grow in that truth. Remember that we have said that truth is dynamic and therefore you will find that the ultimate truth for you is an unfolding of truth and peculiarly true for you. You will find all happiness in that life.

You have time to live your life to its fullest. Often you wish that you had known better or differently earlier. We have explained that truth unfolds itself and this does take time. You have heard the expression that everything happens in its own good time. Accept that this is the case and go and enjoy the freedom that this will afford you.

Go in God's good time and enjoy the wonders of unfolding truth. God blesses you.

SPIRITUAL GROWTH.

We are all doing well. We want to talk about spiritual growth. Nothing in nature grows lineally. Mankind perhaps does not accept this theory. Mankind seeks progression in as straight a line as possible thus defying the natural law.

Think of a tree. Now see yourself as a leaf on that tree. You are the very first leaf on that tree when it is so small that it is difficult for you to see above the surrounding grass. Your world is so small and confined. Time passes and the tree on which you are a leaf grows. Its roots grow deeper into the soil. Its trunk thickens and gets stronger. Its branches begin to spread, and you the first leaf are still there on the top, your world no longer confined, your perceptions no longer inhibited. You are part of the multi-dimensional growth of the tree.

You are born small. You weigh perhaps 3 or 4kg. You may be only 50 to 60cm long. Look at you now. We are only seeing the physical changes that have taken place. Yet the growth we are seeing has indeed been multi-dimensional. Add to this the experiences that are present on a daily basis for you to assist your development. Add to this the deduction you have made around these writings. You begin to learn more about spiritual growth and this in turn increases the dimensions that you grow into. Mankind has a tendency to only consider physical consciousness as a measure of his ability. His intelligence is measured on his ability to regurgitate the imposed rules of others. Education dulls the senses that enable us to see the truth that is for us, and reality becomes unacceptable. This is because Mankind cannot accept the concept of multi-dimensional growth that exceeds the limited perceptions of physical consciousness. After you have read these writings and allowed yourself the time to absorb them do you not feel wiser? Yet you have only been exposed to the truth without a precondition that the truth is limited. The simplicity is that you cannot exist for one moment without growth occurring on all levels. Your physical senses occupy only a small part of the sensorial spectrum. What happens at other parts of that full spectrum cannot physically be experienced as such because of a lack of greater sensitivity. What can however be experienced on a mental level is the comfort of knowing. You will have experienced this.

Knowing is part of the intuitive ability. How often have you known, before some event in your life, the outcome? How often have you ignored this knowing and followed your path to try changing the outcome? How often has this attempt failed? The answer is often. Truth is a major component of intuition. Intuition lets you know the truth of a situation. Trust it.

Spiritual growth for the incarnate being is not restricted by anything. Every experience has the potential to enlighten the being and this enlightenment is in itself growth. This growth can even reflect into the physical world of that being and often they can be seen to glow.

It is inevitable that as we are all a part of the one, that this experience of our communicating with you enables our growth also. We are part of the multidimensional growth of the Spirit and thus we are not necessarily developed greater than you are but we for where we are having this ability to share with you our uniqueness as in this sharing we can share in your uniqueness. We can therefore all grow together.

Our love for you is without question. Our devotion to giving these words is only conditional on your receiving them. All the wisdom exists and if there is no growth towards receiving it, it has no purpose. If there is no growth toward receiving these words, they have no purpose. You give them purpose. For this we thank you.

Go rest in the knowing that you are always within the embrace of God.

HINDSIGHT.

It is constantly confusing as to why hindsight is the greatest reference that mankind uses to justify or condemn some action they may have taken. There is a simplicity that has been missed in this observation. It often is not clear what the consequences of an action may be before that action is taken. The only way to find out is to choose the course of action you wish to take and work positively with the consequences no matter what they may be.

You will see that this appears to carry a risk. There is also a risk in not doing what you feel you should do. So, there is a risk either way and not making your choice does not remove the inherent risk. Think of the person who fears going to the doctor in case they might receive bad news. Whatever news the doctor may have for them, if applied correctly to life, can only be good news. The next step of positive action can be taken.

It is important to realise that God is not vindictive. God does not set traps for you. You do not fall into traps. You find yourself facing the consequences of your own choice and thus you should take on the responsibility for the outcome that comes with hindsight. Hindsight gives you an after view of a situation you have created for yourself. A problem that appears to have been created by a certain action you have taken can present the opportunity of further learning and a greater opportunity of growth in understanding. If you were to look back on a calamity that you experienced over a period of time you will see in hindsight a pattern of action that occurred that caused you hurt or comfort. It is never a question that you should have done things differently. You did what you did by using the available wisdom that you had at the time. Never try and go back and to change the process. You will find that you will only make similar judgements. Apply your experience to your future and you will find that you are sing the additional benefit of the greater wisdom you have gained through the hindsight.

Think of how much truth you have experienced by choice. "I have experienced that and I know", you might say. Feel how strong you are in saying that. Never regret doing whatever it is you have done as the truth gained will mean you do not have to repeat the experience and you can move on. Never think of going back to anything. Realise the phrase "going back" is sufficient to indicate the uselessness of the action of going back. The time that you may want to go back to was a time when you had less experience and less knowledge. Is that where you want to be? You will often hear your fellows talking about the past. It is all right to remember the past, but to live there is to live with the lack of the experience you have gained, in this ever-changing world you have chosen to live in. Always take responsibility for your present state. You got yourself to this state and only you can take yourself on from where you are. There are no shortcuts in acquiring knowledge. Remember that everything is in a sequence and that sequence cannot be broken. It is the law of cause and effect. We in Spirit are here to help you on your way but as a friend. We are not your servants that are to take the burdens from your shoulders. You placed those burdens there and it is for you to learn whether you want to keep them there or not. If you reach a decision, we will help you in achieving the opportunity of testing this decision within the law of cause and effect. When you see occurrences in your life that are running in a very fast sequence then it is obvious that, have you asked us to help you, then we are. We can only work positively with you. If you choose a negative route then you are on your own. You can insist on Spirit help but be aware that if the help you require is against the law and thus take you into negativity, we cannot help you. However, there are those who will offer to help you into negative states but these Spirits are ignorant and really only using you to their own ends.

We will talk more on this another time. Go rest in God's Love.

FORESIGHT.

We have discussed hindsight and how if it is positively applied it can provide a good understanding of how your life at this moment is as it is. If you can reasonably understand why life is as it is, and accept that in a positive form, then it gives you the opportunity of foresight.

Foresight is predictability. It is an ability to predict with reasonability what the future events of your life may hold for you. If you understand the law of cause and effect then you know the saying "as you sow so shall you reap" will let you know that there is a predictable outcome for any action you are about to undertake. In fact, there will be two outcomes possible. One being a positive and the other being a negative outcome. Everybody can apply foresight to their own future. One commodity that you will need will be confidence. Confidence is very important as it will allow you to venture forward whereas if you lack confidence you will dither. You will remember that we spoke of sequence. We said that you have time to measure passing events by. We have sequence, we don't have time.

When you following a spiritual path, you will find sequence takes precedence over time. "Everything happens in its own time". This means that everything has its own place in sequence. If you understand the sequence then you will predict what comes next. Very often man is too engrossed in his life to be able to see what is going on. Man finds himself in the negative sequence of events and is so busy trying to survive the initial error in choosing the future, they can but keep pace with the negative events of life. This survival becomes a habit and all sight is lost of the true mission of life. Life becomes survival and cannot be lived. There will be many opportunities presented to you to remove yourself from the negative spiral, but first you will need to know you are indeed on that downward spiral. Fellow man plays an important role here. Your close friend can look at your life with greater objectivity than you can. If you feel in any way that life seems futile then you must ask your closest friend what they think. They can then be very useful in this way. Your friend will very often speak to you with love and honesty. If you see them as a true friend then you will recognise their lack of personal agenda and their love. You will trust them. Should you accept their offering with openness, it gives us the opportunity to join in and help you into your new and better future

It is very easy to follow the positive sequence or upward spiral. In fact, it is so easy that you tend to just flow along without the recognition and therefore mush of the pleasure of being in the right place at the right time. Again, this indicates that your life lacks objectivity. You will become aware of how wonderful your life is if you also have confidence.

You may ask what confidence has to do with you progress in this latter situation. When life starts to go well for someone, they often fear that this good spell of life won't last – they lack confidence. This lack of confidence causes the person to dither and the sequence is interrupted. It cannot recommence until confidence is restored and the positive application of hindsight and foresight is employed in assessing the way thing can go. When this is successfully applied the positive sequence recommences, and remember we are there with you also.

      Go forward with God's love in and surrounding your heart.

MID-SUMMER.

This day marks the greatest manifestation of the sun, in the solar calendar, in your part of the physical world. It is worth noting that though you perceive that the sun is in your quarter then it is therefore absent from other quarters. The sun is always somewhere not far away.

God is like the sun – always somewhere. Think how it would be if you thought that the sun would never reappear after the night has passed. Yet it will be always there for you so you do not even think about it. Think how warming the winter thoughts are, that summer is on its way. Think of today, the mid-point of summer and how winter approaches from now. You may ask why we require you to think so many things. We ask that you realise that God is but a thought away, and if you to realise this, you will feel the consolation of knowing that indeed God has felt your thought, and He will respond in the most appropriate fashion for you. In the darkest hours of night, you know that sunrise is not far away. In the darkest of life's trials God is not far away. To know that the sun is coming gives a sense of hope and warmth. To know that God is coming gives a hope that exceeds everything you ever thought possible. God's power in your life is only limited by how you think. Do not limit God.

You might find it strange to think that you can limit God's power. God made the law. God gave you free will. If it is your will that God occupies so little of your life then God cannot impose Himself on your living. Therefore, He is "powerless" in your life.

To have light in your life you need firstly to realise its relevance in your life. Nothing in your world can survive without life. The life forms that exist in the dark in your world carry their own light with them. Mankind has that facility also. If man finds himself in darkness, he has the resource of the light within him. If you have experienced such darkness, whether emotionally, spiritually, physically, or even the darkness of night, you will know the comfort that God can be to you. God is in all mankind – usually referred to as the Light Within. When you find that all about you is without any semblance to God then that is where you can call on your inner strength and from that strength re-establish you contact with the all-powerful.

Today we have spoken about the importance of thinking more about God. This thinking will change from conscious thought to eventually become subconscious thought. In any situation of trial, you will then subconsciously think of God and God will be there for you. It is a fact that in any traumatic situation that becomes so intense that you lapse into a semiconscious state and you act automatically, God, with your permission, (given subconsciously), steps in and guides you to the place that the situation requires you to go to. This destination is always the correct place whether you like it or not. God can never take you into a negative situation unless it leads to a positive outcome and restores you to your power. There is no problem presented to you that you cannot overcome. That is God's promise to you. There is no difficulty presented to you that is unnecessary. That is another of God's promises to you.

    Think of God and He is there. Love God and you will feel you are entitled to receive love back from God. God always loves you and wishes only for you to be happy.

NEW AGE MOVEMENT.

One of the sad events of this awakening into Spiritual awareness has been the advent of what is called the New Age Movement. It has been many thousands of years in preparation. The human species had to be evolved in order to present Spirit with a vehicle that was suitable for the task that Spirit needed to perform in order to bring God back into entirety.

In the beginning was the word and the word was God. Do you understand what this saying signifies? It states that the whole universe was contained in one word – God. Such was the power of that word. But power became the word. Everything in nature has its place – not above not below; not superior not inferior; not greater not lesser; not more nor less powerful. We have said before that all species; all aspects of nature are complimentary to each other. If it is necessary to add or take away from that nature then natural order will do just that. We have also told you that nothing is fixed and that everything is a composite part of an evolving whole. All things are equally powerful and therefore do not need the interference of mankind's intellect to disorder it. In the middle of the 19th century Spirit saw that the natural order was ready to accept the dawning of a greater spiritual understanding. If you examine the map of natural order that is contained in the science you know as Astrology you will see that the time was exact for what was to be the dawning of this new age. We have told you that everything in nature is evolving, though the evolvement of a new age is a slow process and not an instant event. You are now further into this new age only because time as you know it has elapsed and events as we see time has occurred. What you do not realise is that the natural order has been delayed by the power hungry in the "new age movement" who through their egos have felt that they know the way. There has been so much misrepresentation of Spirit's intentions that it has taken so long to even get to where you now are and in your time terms that is at least one hundred years behind.

You need to learn the new language. The conventions of religions have stolen the power words and used them to their own ends. You could see that the events of the establishment of religions were in fact the first signs of new ageism and occultism. Now you begin to understand how difficult it has been to find a basis to recommence this Spiritual evolvement. You can see how difficult it is to re-establish the power back to the word and away from the manipulation of mankind. Remember the word is God. If you realise the power of this understanding you will realise that you need no other power. You will expand that understanding continuously. If you were to go on a visit to foreign places you would purchase a guidebook to make you aware of what there is to see. This writing has been your guide to an understanding of the power of the word. Like your guidebook helps you discover a place of interest that evolves into an interesting place as your awareness of that place expands: so too these writing only show you the place of interest and allow you to see what an interesting place it is. You do not need to learn new words. All the words are there. You need to learn their power and proper application in this New World you are entering into.

Go with the word God emblazoned on your heart. Go in Love. Go in peace.

ADVANCEMENT.

Do not be despondent to discover that you may be one hundred years behind. The beauty of spiritual awareness is that it can be instantly achieved. You will have experienced the advent of understanding and how suddenly you discover that you know. The hundred-year gap can be also bridged in an instant with the advent of understanding of what we said when we last communicated.

It is not necessary that we explain further what we have already given to you. You will in time realise the truth of our words. We wish that you develop your spiritual understanding through personal experience and personal understanding of that experience. Should we join you in your endeavours, using your intellect to rationalise what has been said, we would be encouraging your ignorance. If you were to go back to writings that we gave you in this regard you will see what it is we are saying. Have patience and all will become clear. Remember we present the truth for you to discover, not to miss.

Mankind has many frailties. These are mankind's assets not weaknesses. These frailties permit man to err and erring allows experiences to occur that can make man aware. Perhaps it could be said that man's greatest weaknesses are in fact his greatest strengths. You might like to ponder these words for a while before you blindly accept them.

God loves the weak as they offer least resistance to experience. It is often that mankind looks down on the weak with pity and disdain. Man is indeed looking at the nether side of himself and ignorantly refusing to examine the possibility that they are looking at themselves. You have a saying that illustrates this – "there but for the grace of God go I". This should be – "there go I".

This is not a lesson in humility that we are extolling here. These are facts of the impediments to spiritual growth. We see that man is so reluctant to accept their ignorance as a necessary gift to enable positive growth. It is impossible for humankind to acknowledge that they need to learn unless they realise that they do not know. First comes the weakness. This must not be used as an excuse to remain ignorant. It must be used to promote a need to dispel the unknowing. You will often catch yourself perpetrating this particular crime against God. How often have you remained mute, the question behind your lips remaining unasked, your ignorance unchallenged?

It is vital to realise that you have been educated into a greater state of ignorance. You cannot learn until the question is raised. You cannot get the answer until you seek it. Often you accept the truth from other people's perceptions and fail to ask the questions that this, to you, partial truth contains. How often have you found this to be the case? Be honest with yourself. Only you and I will know, and I understand.

Go now and cherish the weaknesses you have. Use them wisely and you will grow so strong spiritually and indeed strong in every way. The truth is so strengthening.

You have God's love. Cherish that love and become wise.

TRUTH (2).

It is sometimes hard for you to accept what it is we wish to impart to you. This feeling you have is because we imply a concept that, because of your preconditioning upsets your mindset. Do not let our words cause you distress, as they are not in contradiction to what you already know. It is, if you like, your knowing will be rearranged into a more logical form – which is sustained by the divine knowledge of truth.

We come in love not in conflict. This is important for you to realise as the truth, in its subtlety, often has difficulty in being obvious. The truth, because it never needs defending, and indeed cannot be defended, needs the opportunity of its questioning to show its validity. Only hindsight conclusively proves the truth.

Again, we stress we come in LOVE and not in conflict. Sometimes our words cause less offence when listened to with this understanding. The fact that we appear to question the truth as seen through the eyes of orthodox religious beliefs and structures does not imply that we condemn or discourage one from pursuing the path of that religion. All that is, is as it is, and therefore must be that way for a good reason so why change it without question?

There is nothing wrong about any religion. We have said that everything is right and this everything includes any religious belief. We do, however, stress that belief is only a transient stage in the development towards truth. The stages are idea, belief, knowledge and finally truth. The idea leads in the quest for an answer to a question that has formed in your mind, whether through an experience or your intuition. You then begin your search for the true answer. In the course of this search, you will encounter many situations or people or, as this quest we speak of is the spiritual quest, a religion that will offer you some answer to your question. This then is the belief that you have been given, or offered for you, to include in the possibilities of the truth you seek. Spirit never speaks definitively. When the truth is offered to you definitively it is not the truth. We have said earlier that the truth is subtle, and can only be proven in hindsight. Therefore, the truth at this stage can only be held as a belief. In your religion or belief frame work you will find that endless questions will arise. These questions arise from your reasoning. The line of questions will have to reach a spiritually logical conclusion before they can cease to be questions. This may take a moment, or a lifetime, perhaps many lifetimes. Remember we have said that Spirit time is sequential and logic reason is a result of sequential questions, one question being answered raising a further question. The result of these questions will be the knowing that you have no further questions to ask. This knowing is definitive truth. You will know something to be true.

The hard part will be that the route you chose to achieve that truth was so long and arduous. You will ask yourself why you were so blind, and indeed many other self-recriminating questions. God will therefore not need to judge your actions. You will judge yourself. Finally, you will come to the conclusion that the reason you had to take the route you took was because it was the one that took you to where you needed to be, and there was no other way. You will appreciate how releasing, how freeing, the truth is. That is there to be appreciated and for you to look forward to. The difficulty is you won't know where or when the true answer is found until you find it – in hindsight.

Go rest and ponder these words. Know when you listen to us you listen to God. We speak for God. These words are lovingly given to us to share with you. Brendan is our medium as we are the mediums for God. Go in His love.

THE CONTROL OF NEGATIVITY.

It is strange to us the way you often hear our words. We have asked you to ponder these words rather than analyse them and compare them to what others have said. We talk about the truth and we have told you that the truth will be found in hindsight. This means that you need not debate nor question our words. You only need to ponder them.

When we come to you it is with your permission. We cannot intrude ourselves into your lives. We cannot control you. Our words must not be used to control anybody. Nobody must use them for this purpose either. We see that we are quoted as a definitive control over others. This is a malpractice. If you should find that you are expected by another to act or perform in a certain manner because that person suggests to you that they have special powers of communication with Spirit, then you will know that they are attempting to usurp the power of God. You will have people who dabble in the psychic areas state that there is only one way for you to travel and that is the way that they claim Spirit has told them that you should take. This person is living in the ignorance and control of negativity. They must not be judged nor condemned. Remember they are not aware that they are so ignorant. Your awareness of their ignorance is all that you need to access the truth of this situation, and therefore to extricate yourself from the intended control. We have told you that your truth is personal to you and therefore cannot be definitively stated by any other.

There is no evil. Evil is a product of the controller who would seek to control through the fear they can generate in you. We say fear not the unknown for the unknown is with us and we know. In other words, we will be there for you, to help answer your questions so that the state of ignorance, you temporarily find yourself in, can be eliminated. We will give you the opportunity to find your truth without you losing any power to us, whereas the controller will always want your power in return for their brand of "illumination". We have said that it is not for you to surrender yourself to God. Why would you allow yourself to surrender to an egocentric mortal?

The indication that you are achieving spiritual understanding is the sense of freedom you will experience. Being in a rule ridden state and controlled state, living a life of fear will show you that, even though you may think that this surrender you have made gives you a sense of security, you still are unhappy with your lot. Contentment comes with knowing. Knowing is to have sufficient answers for the present. The present is then a happy state and you are in your own control

Life for you could be so much happier if you could experience the state that we speak of. Unfortunately, the path that takes you to this happiness cannot be returned to. There is no need to start again, as that would waste all the valuable experiences you have had to date. The difficulty in regaining the path is due to the simplicity that you have been blinded to by the situations and people that have sought to control you. It is hard for you to cast aside the conditioning you have been experiencing all your life. Try to relax yourself into a greater questioning of all that is offered to you to experience. We will endeavour to help you regain a sense of where you are and with the assistance of your questions, we will be able to show you the guidelines that will help you decide where your happiness lies and that then will be the path you seek. It will not be easy though it will be simple – eventually.

Go find your place in God's heart and rest for now.

HOPE (1).

Words we have already given you might have the effect of creating a certain despondency. This is not what we seek to do. Life is not without great hope. Remember that it is not in the interest of anyone that there should not be hope. Hope is invoked when there is an obvious lack of opportunity to success. It is in your darkest hour that you discover hope. Isn't also when you are in your darkest hour that you also discover God. God is hope. We say this because the only certainty you have in moments of trial is that perhaps there is a God who will express His mercy by restoring your life to some semblance of normality. But will He? He won't; but He will be there for you to help you realise that you best not wait any longer but begin the search for the way that your life is directing you. God in His infinite mercy will help you help yourself into the reality that life itself is all that you need, in order to achieve the states of consciousness that will eventually reunite you with the greatness, that is your right as a Spirit, as a part of the very essence of the same God that you plead too in your distress.

So, you see hope is like belief. It is a way of opening yourself to the fact that you can, and will, find your way through the greatest of trials. You will also find that God has set no task greater than your ability to overcome any obstacle that the task presents. The task is there to prove to you that you have the experience, the ability, the knowledge to endure on your own, the trial you are experiencing. Does this feel like "cold comfort" as you might say? It probably does if you do not have hope. It is the same with belief. The threat of dying is a lonely vigil if you have no hope of an afterlife. Life is so empty without the belief in God. Life is hopeless without the belief that God will be there for you in your trial.

Do you believe in God? This question is one for you to ponder upon and not to answer. Do you have a sense of hope? Are you optimistic about your future? Do you feel you have a future? Have you eventually realised why we ask these questions? It does not matter if you believe in God or not. Not believing in God will only invite the experience that will give you the knowledge of God. If you dismiss the opportunity that the potential of God's existence will give you, you will not solve your dilemma. If you believe that there may be a God you stand a greater chance of having the glory of that truth shown to you. If you do not at least believe you will be presented with the experience that will most certainly raise the question of your lack of belief and the resulting answer will bring you to the stage of awareness that will suggest that there is more to life than there first appeared to be. The uniqueness of God is what we talk about. The divine plan is so complete that it is easy to arrive at a position in life where your development as a spiritual being becomes an enjoyable task rather than a trial.

This is why we speak of hope this night. Life without hope is a trial. We want to show you how by using hope, optimism, belief and questions you can find that the glory of a full and fruitful life can be yours.

We do not feel that any individual is so far from the truth. Some people feel that they are far from the truth but this is because they are not looking to the side of life that presents the opportunity of true Love and true Light.

Test our words. See if by doing nothing, other than to ponder, you discover that your life can change in a positive way. With you not doing anything how can life change? You are not lifeless. You are doing something. You are testing our words. We don't do anything either. Our words are true, truth does it all. That is the law. When you create the space for opportunity to occur, it happens. It's as simple as that.

Trust in God. Go with hope.

MIRACLES.

It is wonderful that hope for happiness always exists for those who have the awareness that God is indeed good. God rewards those who seek to live the life of a spiritual being incarnate. This state is often neglected in preference to a life as an incarnate being without an awareness of their Spirit. It is not that God expresses preferential treatment on His followers. The system that God has put in place through His creation is such that it automatically rewards – by life being happy and fulfilled, and punishes by the transgressor suffering the effects of what they have caused for themselves. We have talked of the law of cause and effect.

We want to help you understand how you can become the recipient of all the goodness that God has provided for you in His creative process. We have told you that God does not await your demise and arrival in heaven so that He may judge you and punish you or reward you for the way that you have lived your life. There is no necessity for Him to do so as the law has already been invoked and life and what you call after life will carry the consequences of your behaviour.

The realisation that this life is a spiritual journey provides you with the means of presenting you with the opportunity of daily miracles. The reason that you do not expect a good life is why your life tends to be laborious. If you are to learn that you can expect a good life then you will be able to take the opportunity of having one. Miracles are a daily occurrence. You are unaware of them because they are tending to happen for other people and not you. The occurrence of a miracle in your life usually is dismissed as a coincidence. Watch out for a miracle. In your watching out you will need to provide for the opportunity for it to happen. A miracle is a positive happening. It cannot happen in space where negativity exists. Negativity and positivity do not mix. You therefore need to create a positive space for the miracle. You cannot have a positive space if you entertain the negative thought, "it will never happen for me". You need to adopt the attitude that anything is possible and, provided it is good for you, will happen at the right time and in the right way. This brings us to the next problem you are likely to encounter. This is where another negative form of thinking takes place. While you are awaiting your miracle, you must avoid predetermining what form or in what way this miracle might manifest itself. A miracle is the unexpected taking place in an unexpected way. How then do you think you can guess how a situation will work out? If you thought that you had the answer you wouldn't need the miracle. To have a miracle in your life you first need to realise that you are in a dilemma that you have no solution to. You generally will have tried all in your power to resolve the situation but to no avail. You consciously hand your problem to God. This hand over is only temporary, as God will have to return it to you to solve the difficulty you are having. Remember it is your experience and this experience is to help you understand the power you have and not the power God has. You put the problem temporarily in God's hands and it is for you then to reassess your life's potential from the perspective of its current state. The options that life offers must all be considered from the positivity that can be gained. This is spiritual positivity we talk of. While you are considering your life and seeking to find a happier direction to take God will also have been busy setting the wheels in motion for your miracle to occur. When synchronicity is achieved, that is when you, your life and God's plan all coincide, the miracle occurs. The miracle is placed along the road of life for you to encounter. Waiting for it to happen will mean that you will inevitably remain in the wrong place. You need to be making progress in order to arrive at the correct place in life for your happiness to begin. When you get there, God will hand you back your problem at a time you can resolve it and often with a wonderful bonus. For example, you will no doubt already in your life experience an increase in your financial welfare at a time when an unexpected bill arrives. That is a miracle. There is no law against seeking material gain. God realises that the medium of money is important to the running of lives in the material world you exist in at this time. That is why it is all right to ask God for financial assistance. Remember that it must always be for your good, otherwise God cannot help you.

Go test our word and experience a miracle. The miracles that become an everyday occurrence become a miraculous way of living. Happiness exists and life becomes fulfilled. You must accept that this responsibility is yours alone and the decision you make is what changes your life's potential for all to be well. Spiritual success is your goal.

God blesses you.

MAKING PROGRESS.

We spoke to you on the subject of miracles and how you can introduce them in an everyday way into you life so that life itself is one long happy miracle. This is the way your life should be. If you keep this idea as your goal then you will achieve it. You must not put yourself under any pressure in attempting to achieve this state as that pressure in itself will cause restrictions in the implementation of your personal Divine Plan.

We like to see you progress. We do not see you when you drop behind your potential. Let us explain. We cannot look back. Once we move forward, we cannot go back. That is positive potential. We are in view of our destiny and therefore have no desire to digress from that goal. We have explained to you before that though we may guide you, our level of consciousness is such that at the times we are your guide we are only a few steps further forward than you are. In this way we are better attuned to your needs. It is in our interests that you progress continuously as this allows us to attain our "higher" spiritual status and that is such a pleasant state that we would share it with you should you permit yourself to join us. It is always in your interest that you acknowledge that this state is for you. When we spoke of the introduction of miracles into your life it is closely related to this blissful state we refer to. There is no comfort in austerity, penance, or any negativity of that nature. This is why we suggest that sacrifice is unnecessary. That is a negative state.

Back is negative and that is why we cannot go in that direction and remain positive. When you regress, we lose sight of you. When we lose sight of you, we wait for you to return to sight. You achieve this by seeking your path and this in turn brings you back into contact with us. We do not have time so it is no great inconvenience for us to wait whether it be minutes, days or years. Do not distress yourself at the thought of your delaying our progress.

We would recommend to you that "back" should not be a choice for you either. Proceed from where you are. It is simple. If you realise that you have been digressing then you have actually progressed to the point where you began to digress. So there is no need to backtrack.

Life is wonderful no matter where you spend it. It is full of possibility and hope. That you are in the physical world or in the Spirit World makes little difference. We live with the same prospect of hope as you do. There is a difference however and that is that we have had the benefit of the conscious experience of death of our physical bodies. You do not have this experience in your conscious memory however and the threat of that experience will act as your guidance perhaps more than any other fear you may have. The instinct of human survival is precedential to you. We will be talking on this topic later but for now we would like to tell you that the human experience is not unpleasant and with the knowledge that there is a continuance of life, albeit in a different form than you occupy at present, it is not a strange feeling to be in your Spirit form. It is a familiar feeling but does take a little adjustment in order to invoke that memories of previous Spirit existence. You will get plenty of assistance from all your friends when you arrive here.

Do not fear death. Unfortunately, mankind has used the human fear of death as a tool to control with. The threat of murder, of war are typical of this way. Remember death has many forms and really is just the ending of a phase in your eternal existence but not only that, it represents the potential of a birth into the next phase. If you have found that you understand the potential of positive progress this change will be looked forward to by you and not feared. If you were to know that death carries no pain and that it releases you into a new and better existence you would not have the reluctance to experience death.

You are not about to die. That is not why we speak of death this time. To Spirit death holds no mystery. Go rest in God's Love knowing that all is well with you and for you.

ABOUT DEATH.

We were talking about death the last time we communicated. This is a subject that seems to disturb humankind. We in the Spirit world see it as the return to totality as we know it. To be part of the Spirit world with the awareness that goes with this closeness to God allows us to feel more a part of the total being than is possible whilst incarnate. It is very difficult for a Spirit when it is in the flesh to disconnect itself from the senses that pervade the combined consciousness that makes up the mind of the human being. When the Spirit returns to this world it celebrates as it is really a return home.

Can you imagine what it would be like for the Spirit if it had to remain in your world with a physical body that continues to deteriorate until it has no means to function with? That is not a pleasant thought is it? A Spirit in your world that finds itself trapped in a body that has ceased to function perhaps through some accident knows where it is and that if necessary, any suffering it might be experiencing will be ended through the facility of dying. Death is necessary for the living. How else can this world be accessed on a more permanent basis. We know that meditation gives you a temporary access to this world. You know when you experience this world that the beauty leaves you with a certain satisfaction and a hunger for more experiences of this kind. You will have difficulty in conveying your feeling of the experience to others unless they too have experienced a visit to the Spirit world. It is such a wonderful place to visit and even better to live in and yet in your meditation you have only stepped inside the door of this world.

It is a pity that more people don't visit us as they would have less of a fear of what might or might not await them when they eventually take the journey home. Most people, when they die, successfully make the transition. There are some that have difficulty and need great assistance. The most common causes of difficulty are the hard held beliefs that the soul carries with it into this world, and cannot recognise the truth because of these beliefs. Let us clarify what the difference is between the Spirit and the soul. The body we know to be the physical being and this physical being has what could be best described as an invisible membrane between it and its Spirit. It is like the membrane inside the shell of an egg. This membrane is what you call the soul. When the physical body is shed at death this soul form remains around the Spirit to give it a form that would be recognisable to those already in the Spirit world waiting for their friends and loved ones to join them. In this way when the Spirit re-enters this world there will be members of their ancestral clan waiting to greet them. The ancestors will also don a recognisable mantel so that the newcomer can recognise them also. Where this system breaks down is where the newly deceased insists that it must enter the Spirit world "body and soul". The body has much emphasis placed upon it by those who mourn the passing of the deceased and in this way the Spirit is held back in the physical world by the poorly informed or educated consciousness of the soul. The deceased therefore tends to stay close to the body they have just vacated, unaware that their journey cannot proceed until they realise that there is more to this business of dying than immediately meets the eye. Should they see the form of an ancestor they will think they have seen a ghost and run from it. They have not the ability to advance further into the Spirit world because they have no perception that it exists. They look back to where they have been – back to the physical world – and see the ignorance of others of like mind. These other minds lend no hope to the salvation of this lost soul. There is a great need for humankind to be enlightened to the correct understanding of death.

As we have indicated there is no pain in death. Indeed, it is the opposite – death often releases one from the pain. The actual transition is very fast. It is very similar to the body waking from the sleep conscious state into the physical conscious state. You will have experienced the confusion of awakening especially if you have been having an intense dream. For the first few moments of being awake you are still trying to relate your dream state to this world you have awoken too. If there is somebody with you this helps you to stabilise your thoughts and realise where you are. So too on your entry to this world there are those you will recognise waiting to help you stabilise your consciousness and attune to this world. They will take you into your new-found home and assist your adjustment to being a Spirit once again. When you make this transition to being a Spirit all your Spirit abilities and functions will return. You will see your friends in their "true light", their Spirit form, and you will no longer need the soul membrane. This is when you will feel truly free. There is more to tell you of this world but that is for another day. Be not afraid of death. Have a good life away from this fear. Death will come in its own good time. We've been there so we know.

Go rest in the assurance that God certainly loves you and wishes you no harm. With this assurance know that God has no cruel fate awaiting you. God blesses you.

ANIMALS AND DEATH.

We will continue with our conversations around the subject of death. Life cannot be discussed without discussing death. The process of Spirit evolvement includes both so therefore an understanding of the roles of both need deliberation.

Humankind looks down of members of the animal kingdom as being less than humankind in value or status. This is a common ignorance carried by, unfortunately, most of the human race. If something is "evil" it very often carries the symbol of a snake or some such. If something is dirty the symbol of the fly is often attached. These creatures are all part of the Divine Creation and therefore must be of God. In the understanding of that which is of God there is also the understanding that all parts of creation are embedded with the imprint of the creator. Animals therefore do possess a Spirit and because they have an incarnate, physical body also have soul. The arrogance of humankind denies the human the positive opportunity to learn from the experiences of the animal. Remember that the experience of one is also the experience of any who share whatever that experience is, in whatever aspect they share. Humankind is animal in its physical sense. This association with all living things needs to be recognised before true harmony can exist in your world. How humbling it is for you to realise that you share that world of yours on an equal basis with the fly and the snake and indeed the pig. You are neither more nor any less important no matter how you may think you have improved yourself beyond them.

Like humankind animals survive death or should we say that their soul and Spirit survive death in the same way that humankind experiences it. They too have the opportunity of continuous evolvement. Some have even experienced the life of a human being. You can also make this choice to incarnate in human animal form, and maybe you already have experienced the life of a dog or cat etc. You will often experience the presence of your departed pet, and the surviving pets you may have will show the signs that they also can see or sense that same presence. It is comforting to know that they are there for you, waiting. It is also comforting to know that the reason they would wait for you is their response to the love and understanding you afforded them while they shared life with you. Every creature you have shown kindness to will be there to return that kindness to you when you return to the Spirit World. You have been told that you cannot take anything with you when you die and here is one thing that has been stored for you to return to, kindness.

This introduces the problem of meat eating. There are other animals besides the human that eat meat. Why then should it be different? If you are aware that the design of creation includes the supply of food for the animals to share in, including the meat of other animals, then you must see that your instincts to consume various foods will often carry the desire to eat meat. The problem is that there is a difference between slaughter and sacrifice. The Spirit who decides to incarnate into a form that will supply the food chain makes the sacrifice. This Spirit puts its physical form forward for consumption. Other animals eat humankind. Some humans choose to be buried in the soil and thus feed a host of other creatures. Do not let this thought disturb you. You will have no personal experience of being consumed.

We hope that you will understand that the nature of living is all to do with birth and death and that it is a wonderful, complete plan that unfolds for all. We do not want you to find that we enjoy the details of the dying process, as we do not want you to fear the same process. God has designed this and it should hold no fears for you if you know God the way we do.

Go in Love and Peace and in the knowing that God has only good things for you.

DYING—A PAINLESS PROCESS.

We have talked about death and now we would like to enlighten you to the experience of dying. Many people seem to fear the dying process and do not realise that it is a painless process. You are aware that when a person undergoes surgery, they are anaesthetised so that they do not feel the pain of the surgeon's scalpel. The anaesthetic alters the patient's consciousness away from the pain sensors. For some time after the operation the patient is under the influence of the drug and when that wears off the pain returns. The process of dying is somewhat similar.

Imagine a person who is suffering from a disorder that is causing them terrible pain. The pain could be so bad that they feel death would be preferable, even with the fear they might have around it. On the physical conscious level, they fear but on a spiritual level they know that the relief will come when they detach from the physical body. Spirit does not experience pain. The only suffering a Spirit can experience is the absence of God's

Love. The further the Spirit is from God the weaker is the feeling of that Love. In the physical body the Spirit can experience all the emotions associated with that pain that the body is feeling. That person in that pain cannot translate their feelings into spiritual understanding because firstly, they do not always have the spiritual education to correctly analyse and secondly, the pain is so intense that they cannot rise above it. When that person can understand the cause and experience of their disability then they can make rational choices to recover from the malady or to choose the alternative of dying. This decision can only be made on a spiritual level of consciousness. Whatever the choice, it is generally found that the pain diminishes with the understanding. Should the decision be to die then the observer will see peace come over the dying person as their consciousness alters into its spiritual state and often the dying person will see some of their friends who are already in the Spirit world calling to them in reassurance. All this can be disconcerting to the observer should they not have the experience of knowing about death. Where there is knowledge about death Spirit can more easily leave the body and also Spirit can help more in the after-death process.

There is relief from pain in death. The pain remains in the physical world and particularly with those who have to continue in life without their loved one. If they were to know the peace and happiness that their dearly departed is experiencing, they would get such comfort. The observer remembers the body's reaction to the feeling of pain and sometime if the body struggles to resist the Spirit leaving it, they can often suffer great anguish at the apparent distress that their loved one suffered. Their loved one did not suffer. The body is similar to a mechanical device that is programmed to react in certain ways to certain stimulation. Even in death it will react. It takes some time before the physical energy totally discharges and the physical body goes into total repose.

Know that death is only a transformation from one temporary state of consciousness to the real consciousness of Spirit. Would that you would come to us more often and experience our world, your 'to be' world, you would better understand. We cannot use your words to describe our world or indeed to do justice to the invaluable process that creation has designed called the dying process.

There is no pain in death. You do not feel your last breath leaving your body. You do not experience the judgement of God. You do not face the punishment for misdeeds. You will meet those you love and who have loved you. You will experience freedom as you have never experienced in your earth life. You will experience the truth in a very viable way. You will love being here. You will want to go back to earth to tell all your friends how great it is. This latter is where we come into the picture – because that is what we're doing.

God blesses you.

THE SPIRIT WORLD.

We wish to attempt to describe this world to you. We have once before described this world as a world of what you would term fantasy. Many of your writers have had to ascend into the world of fantasy in order to create a picture that represents utopia. The degree of perfection that can be envisaged by this practice is unbelievable. You see we are already into the concept that the conditions you will encounter are very difficult to believe. We have also said that belief is only a part of the way to the truth. For you to experience this truth will necessitate your totally entering this world.

We have suggested that meditation it a good way of reaching the doorway into this realm. You will have read that Jesus would lead his disciples into the Kingdom and how they experienced the ecstasy of that encounter. That Jesus brought them to the doorway in meditation and enabled them to glimpse into this world and to get a taste of the happiness and joy that exists here. You also can have that experience. You can also have the experience of meeting those whom you loved when they were sharing your world with you. Naturally you cannot stay here for any length of time because you have to complete your life there first, but it is nice to know that this world is here for you to return to. People who practice meditation and gain a greater experience will describe it as returning home. This is indeed what it is. This is the home of your immortal self, the home of your Spirit.

You might ask what we do all day. We do not have day; we do not have night. What we have is continuous happiness. To help you understand we would like to compare your daily existence with our life here. When you have a good day and are happily enjoying yourself you will wish the day never ends. We see you getting tired but you still persist in getting the last ounce of enjoyment out of the day. You use stimulants in order to sustain your energy levels and thus stretch your limits. We have no tiredness and our day never ends. We have boundless energy. We have an uncluttered imagination. We can create our world to enable us to continue our happy pursuits. We have a greater clarity as to satisfying our needs. We know that we have survived death (often our greatest mortal fear). Are you getting an idea of our world? We want to share this happiness with you but if you reject our suggestions as being too fantastic then you cannot share.

Fantasy is easy to destroy. You just stop believing and it's gone. This is why there are more pessimistic people. This is why there so many depressed people. They suffer the sense of hopelessness that is fuelled by the lack of fantasy. Children see so many possibilities for their own futures provided they are allowed by the adult to fantasise. How often their dreams are crushed by the disillusioned adult telling them that the fantasy they are engaged in is not part of the real world. Yet the world we live in is the real world and is a world of fantasy. Is it not possible that the child has a greater sense of the real world and that the adult can learn to seek the potentials that the child's fantasy can expose the adult to it? It's the adult who is losing out and who is showing their ignorance by not sharing in the child's gift. The child soon stops dreaming and the illusion turns into disillusion. The child grows into the depressed adult with no hope of living, only the hope of surviving, it's potential to create a happy life destroyed.

Think of this. Allow yourself to seek the dream that can make you happy. Allow yourself to fantasise. It is a wonderful place to be and a very spiritual place to be - provided you invite us into your thoughts. We can then share our views of the life we have. Remember to us the real life is here in this fantasy land and this world is no illusion except to those who refuse to acknowledge that there is a kind loving God who as the creator of everything has prepared this world of continuance so that we may be eternally happy.

Go rest in His Love and dream on.

LIVING.

We have spoken of death, now let us talk about living. It is often said that in order to live one has to experience the pain of death. When one discovers that there is no pain in the final stages of the process of death then the fear is released and the living begins. See how a person who is diagnosed as terminally ill changes their attitude to the life they have been living and strike out to get what it is they most wanted from life before it's too late. It is a pity that such extremes had to be reached before they would decide to do this. Life is there for the living at all times but it is up to the individual to live it. How many subject themselves to a life of servitude to a system which is at it's very best corrupted by power seeking.

This is what we wish to discuss this time. Humankind constantly seeks to develop but only within the parameters decided by those who are in control. Humankind is unaware of the agenda that the system has nor is the system aware of its own agenda. Where does the corruption come from? The corruption comes from those who control the system. And who controls the system? Now that is a very good question. You are part of the system and the system is in place for you. You might ask why then does it not do you any favours? The reason for this ineffectiveness in your favour is because you are not in control. The system of living in the western world was devised by civilisations that existed long ago. These civilisations devised a system that controlled the masses for the benefit of the few in control. Modern philosophy is based on the reason that these civilisations expounded in exercising the control and thus modern society is governed by a system based on an out-of-date philosophy. You can take control of your own life and indeed you have a duty to yourself to do so. This does not mean that you have to walk over your fellow humankind but it does require you to be conscious of your own feelings in relation to living and your need in that. If you do not exercise your rights in relation to your feelings then what is the point of having feelings or a point of view. We have talked before about individuality. In your exercising your response to your feelings you express to the world your point of view – provided that response is not controlled by the system. If it is controlled it is a conditioned response in favour of the system. You have heard and maybe even taken part in mind control courses. These are courses to condition your response to a given situation. It is not your individuality that is expressed rather the safe option in favour of the controller. And that isn't living.

So what is living? One word that could be used for this is freedom. The freedom we speak of is the right and will to clearly express our response to your feelings and points of view without the fear of criticism or censure. Think what it is in life that you are unhappy about and what it would take to make the necessary changes to your life to make it happy or happier. What is it that is stopping you from achieving that happiness? Whatever that is represents the first task you need to undertake in order to begin living. You will find that the journey to your goal will be more interesting than the achievement of reaching your goal. When you do reach your goal you will then realise that it is not your final destination but the first part of a very long sequence of events that will stretch to the end of this life and beyond into the next as this life is but a part of this sequence that started so long ago. It does get better but you will have to wait to see where you have been before you can fully appreciate the wonders of life. It is the same as you waiting till the night before you can assess the day you have had.

Go rest in God's love and look forward to life and living it.

CONTROL BY LIMITATION.

You have heeded our words and you will find that life can begin afresh. That is if you did heed our words! We feel that humankind cannot so easily accept the words that we give without imposing their preconditioning. This is not intended to suggest that we judge you from afar. It is that we understand that you have difficulties that you need to acknowledge.

We have talked before about the limitations that are imposed upon humanity by the systems that they seek to live under. These limitations are often disguised as security. You have had, in your world, nations that are basically held captive by the governing authority. Nations where you would need to obtain permission to leave: nations indeed where you have to seek permission to visit: where is the freedom in that? Humankind is so unaware of many of the boundaries that are imposed. Then there are the daily limitations. How free are you? You need to rise from your bed at a certain hour in order to carry out the daily duties that you have committed yourself to. Again, we stress that we do not sit in judgement dictating what you should or should not do. We talk of these things to draw your attention to the lack of freedom that you are subjected to and often without your realising that you are not a free person. Your world, in order to control you, suggests that you accept that certain situations are normal. Should you decide that you cannot accept this, society has to produce a label for you that adequately describes you and pigeon holes you into a category that does not threaten the control. They have labels such as "conscientious objector", "eccentric" and of course lunatic, that enable the system to direct the "abnormal" to a place where they cannot weald any power that might challenge the ignorance of the "system". Your world enjoys misery in some perverted misunderstanding. Good news doesn't satisfy the masses and therefore the media feeds bad news. Every day you are exposed to a fresh threat usually caused by the mismanagement by the system. We know that we paint a bleak picture of your world for you. It is your responsibility to encourage change in this control system so that there is an understanding of good news and that it doesn't threaten the system. The system has been established and become fixed long ago. It is time for it to change.

You can change the system. There is a business idiom of supply and demand. If you question what your needs are and then seek to supply those needs you will often find that the system has not the means to fulfil your needs. You must demand this fulfilment and should you find that your demand is not met you must pursue your objective of fulfilment. This is where spiritual awareness can be helpful. We have said before that revolution is not necessary. If you thought that this is what we are suggesting then you will see that you have introduced a limitation to the potential effectiveness of that which we speak. We have said that you can be guided by happiness. Remember there can be no compromise in the solution that provides your happiness otherwise there will be another limitation – the limitation of unresolved issues that impede progress until they are resolved. Be sensitive to how you feel and go by those feelings. If it doesn't make you feel happy don't do it. If you feel compelled to still do it knowing it will not make you happy, understand the compromise that has occurred to make you do something that you do not want to do. Do not then allow yourself into the limiting situation that caused this problem in the first place. There is nothing in your world that has the right to overrule your feelings. That you should be asked to do so should make you wary of the one who asked you. Beware those that use the guise of having "special powers" to suggest to you they can help you take back the control in your life. Understand that the choice is yours alone and that you have all the power you need to make these decisions yourself. Spirit cannot over rule your feelings. You can allow a Spirit to do so but that then removes the precious power from you and endows the controlling Spirit with that power. You can then become increasingly dis-empowered by that Spirit until it has the control over you that it requires. So too with the system it will offer you situations that are enticing and when you empower it to the position where it needs to be it ignores the promises it made to entice you to empower it and uses the power you gave it to its own ends – usually to your cost.

Think upon these words. Apply them to your daily life. See how restricted you are in the ability to access happiness. See how it is that subservience is the "easier" route for you to take. See how the subservient route leads you towards a tolerance of unhappiness. Question yourself regarding the choices you have made and then seek the opportunity to redirect your energy into re-solving your difficulties. Change is always a good thing provided you do it for the best reasons and for no other reason.

We will talk more about this. Go live a life of constant change for the better – get happier for your sake. That is all God wishes of you. In other words, get happier for God's sake.

Take our Love for you.

REINCARNATION.

We shall talk about reincarnation. This is a topic that causes many questions to be asked. There is reincarnation. Earth life form or indeed any life form other than Spirit life form is totally unnecessary without the needs of Spirit to evolve. It really doesn't matter whether you accept reincarnation or not but it is good to consider the potential this facility offers to the evolving Spirit.

The physical form exists as a means to transport a Spirit through the various experiments and trials it needs in order to gain a greater understanding of its individual function in the totality that is God. If the Spirit sees that it requires particular experiences then it will choose the appropriate vehicle for the journey. In your physical state you make similar decisions regarding the transport most appropriate to your needs. Your Spirit chose your physical being for its course in evolvement at this time in its migration back to completeness.

There is little doubt that you have been here before. At this stage there are no new Spirits being created even though some might opine that there are. God was one. God is still one but at this moment is awaiting you and I and so many other aspects to reunite with Him again. I use the term Him out of lack of vocabulary to address God otherwise. God is neither male nor female as you might like to see Him. He possesses the energy that you classify as male and female but that is all. I have no gender nor do I have a name or title but I will hear you address me in the terms that best suit the impression that you have of me.

It is the choice of the individual as to whether they reincarnate or not. They are not sentenced to a life of misery because of the terrible sins they performed against whatever. This is a free choice and the exercising of free will. You will not really understand the true value of the physical form until you are back in this world. The value of the incarnation will also have to wait until your return to the Spirit world before it can be appreciated. Never doubt that this will be the case. If you feel that you have made a complete mess of your earth life then this is as valuable and having made a complete success of it. Either way you succeed. If you make a complete mess and don't realise it, this is only because you haven't finished making the mess yet. If you were to find yourself in this latter state you will not have arrived with the understanding that you can reincarnate. There is even a possibility that you won't even know you are dead. You therefore cannot return to the physical world until you are wise enough to wish that return. No evil Spirit can thus be incarnated in a physical form. No one is born evil.

Sometimes it might appear as though there are evil people in your world and that they are manifestations of the devil. There is no devil as such, there is however the negativity that is created by humankind that can sometimes take on devilish proportions. There are Spirits who sometimes take on the role that puts them into a position that appears to display extreme negative traits. Their physical form may perform acts that are seen by humankind as being extremely evil. The Spirit that takes on this role is a very brave Spirit and can run the risk of severe spiritual trauma and sometimes remain stuck in the role they played even after the physical body has been shed. It is important to these Spirits that humankind does not judge them too harshly, rather that humankind take the task of understanding the positive lessons from these apparently negative situations or events. In this way the troubled Spirit can see the positive value that it has contributed to the whole task of evolvement. Some Spirit has to do the dirty work.

Go rest and ponder these words. Understand that all is for your good as all good comes from God. We could also add that all badness also comes from God for your good.

God blesses you.

JESUS.

There was a reason for our discussion on reincarnation. This time we wish to speak of the being you call Jesus. Many have raised the question of who this person was and many have used this name to their own ends and not in the correct intention that Jesus would have liked. It is unfortunate that the words of this one have been used mainly to further the cause of many individual's ego and not in the promotion of the consciousness of God.

We have spoken before of the misappropriation of the power of the word and now we will speak of the misappropriation of the power of the being and personality called Jesus. Jesus and reincarnation are connected. Let us explain. We have said that the decision to reincarnate rests solely with the Spirit who seeks to do so. There are many here who would be called by you a teacher. These Spirits are not more evolved but evolved into that area which is more suited to the role of teacher. We have explained how this communicator is an accumulation of essences. A teacher is also an accumulation of many essences and each essence is important to the accumulative knowledge of the teacher. The collective essences can still be called a Spirit as is has no mass and therefore is neither larger nor smaller than any other Spirit.

The Spirit who chose to incarnate in the body that was named Jesus had been in many other incarnations and is still in your world incarnate. He is still teaching but not as you would know him as you can only identify with the legend. He has been, (and we use the word He as it would be preferable than he/she/it), in your world in many guises. Throughout your history he appears many times with different names and forms and at different times. As we have said he is there with you in a different form and with a different name but he is still doing the same work as teacher. You must not seek him, as you would be wasting your time, you would not recognise him. If his teachings reach you, you will have done all that is necessary, and he will have done that which he has sought to do – bring humankind into greater awareness of God.

If you listen to the words spoken by him in his incarnation when he was Jesus you will realise that he spoke continuously of God his father. God is the father of us all and when we realise this, we can begin to be part of the greater family of Spirit. Jesus thought the way. He never suggested that he was going to carry you on his back. He helped people with their difficulties but could never de-power the benefit of their individual experiences by releasing them from the responsibilities.

We have spoken last time how some Spirits choose to live a life that to some might appear as evil. Jesus to some people is more of an anti-Christ rather than the Christ. To others he appears more human and then again as superhuman to some. Jesus was human; his Spirit was superior to human – just like you. There were those who deified Jesus so that they as his "friend" would in turn be raised in the estimation of other humans. By turning Jesus into a God allowed many who promoted his cause as a God to become saints or some such. If there is no hierarchy in Spirit how is it that the Christian church needs to have such a system? The answer is obvious and contained in one word – power. The power of experiencing the truth is unknown to those who seek the power of Jesus. They have misheard his words.

We hope you will not misread our words likewise. We seek to enlighten you not to cause conflict within your mind. We suggest that if our words contained in this communication offend or disturb you then you stop reading them now and reread what has been already been written. You can then commence reading our words again should you wish.

We come in the name of God to bring you a greater experience of who you are, and to unburden you of the false goals and rules that have been suggested to you by those who seek to keep you in servitude to a system or belief, that serves only those whom you allow into a power over you. They are not God. God has no servants. God has many parts all working in a totality. You are one of those parts. You are part of God.

God is Love.

PSYCHOLOGICAL BARRIERS.

We come now to the main purpose of our recent visits. We have been concentrating on breaking down the psychological barriers that have been in place for so many generations of humankind. It is a difficult task for us to perform as these barriers are so well entrenched. Remember we cannot overstep the rules of free will. We cannot control you. We can help you become aware through the teaching that we have imparted and through the questions that we have helped you form and ask. The answer to any question is not finite when this answer comes from Spirit. Do not accept any answer that we may provide as being finite. You can accept that it is the answer for that moment and should you keep that question always available for asking, then you can enjoy the answers you will receive as they unfold. This is the dynamics of truth.

We have told you of the one called Jesus. He came to your world in the light of truth. He came to teach through enlightenment. He sought neither glory nor acclaim. There were those who were waiting for a saviour and there were those who felt they had no need for salvation. There were those who needed a leader to take control of their lives and give them a better environment free from the rule of Rome. There were those who wanted to be free from the rule of the Jewish faith. When Jesus appeared in the midst of these diverse needs each form of need sought in this man a purpose that would satisfy itself. Some succeeded in finding some solace and some didn't. Those that found something that would be of assistance to them glorified the person of Jesus and those that didn't find what they expected condemned him. The difficulty with appearing as a saviour is that the expectations of those who seek to be saved have to be satisfied. These expectations are such that there can be no saving. If these expectations were acceptable then salvation would already have taken place. If salvation hadn't taken place then the expectations were not accurate and whether Jesus or God were to make them true then the expectations could not be right, and that the assumption that there was positive Divine intervention would have been an illusion created in the ignorance of the needy. You are warned of false prophets and we would also like to add the awareness of false devotees. Many rally around the man called Jesus so that their belonging to this group will guarantee them salvation. They do not question and personalise the truth of their position and in this way give into a blind faith usually through the fear of losing the position of belonging. They are afraid of being outside. They become the false devotee. The one they revere as the prophet cannot control this state of that being. The deified teacher can only continue to teach. They must be aware all the time of the position they hold and not think that because they help others become aware that they are something special. Others may seek to put them on a pedestal. That is where those people will see them. The teacher must keep their feet always on the ground and know that. This in time will allow the misguided to see the folly of their own ignorance and to reassess their beliefs, hopefully finding the truth. Unfortunately, the ignorance is such that the false devotee does not realise the responsibility they have to themselves and that all that is happening in life is for their good should they accept that they have through their own action created the necessity of the experience. They usually apportion blame to the teacher or to the deity if things go wrong. They think God is cruel because God allows somebody die. They do not think of the one who dies as exercising their will and realising that they have achieved their purpose from their life and decided that now is the time to move on. They do not want to accept that earth life is but a small part of evolvement. They do not want to accept the responsibility of their own choices in this incarnation and that should they achieve their goal they will also have that choice of going home to God. Jesus continuously gave hope through the work that he did. There is no complete unbiased record of his work so it is difficult for you to touch the truth of what is recorded. We have said that the expectations of the masses that were exposed to his teachings had such diverse needs that their satisfaction or disappointment can be reflected in any report that might exist. It is what his words and teaching mean to you that will give you access to the power of being yourself. Any confirmation you receive that makes you aware of your own knowing is an endorsement of the power of the teaching of any prophet. It must be your own truth untainted by the influence or bias of any other.

No prophet is God. No God is non-Spirit. No God is complete until all components that make this God are reassembled. You are one of those components who through your seeking will find your way back into the completeness. There is only one God composed of many parts, each part unique in its function within the total Being. You are one of those parts. That part is your immortal Spirit, your God part.

Spirit – Teachings From The Highest Source

Go nurture that part through Love.

MORE ON JESUS.

We have more for you on the subject of Jesus. Jesus did not incarnate with the purpose of establishing a new religion. It was the power seeker that did this. It was the purpose of the incarnation of Jesus that he teaches the fundamentals of spirituality. If you are to examine the fundamentals of all religions you will find that they are all similar. They are spiritually based but differ on dogma. Dogma is the control on the religion and on the followers of that religion. Why is there a need to differ if fundamentally all religions are the same? Why are there so many different names for God if there is only one God? Why is there the suggestion of false God's if there is only one? Why is your God the right one and is it different from all others beliefs? Go back to the fundamentals and restructure your spiritual truths without the intrusion of control of religion. Do you feel nervous about this idea? If you do then you really need to look at your sense of self-confidence. Do you not feel confident that you have the truth in your life? Remember that we have spoken of truth before and you might like to examine again the words we gave you on this. No religion can give you the truth. The truth is contained within every religion – in its fundamental state. The specific truth that any religion can give you is only for you to begin the search for your specific truth, a truth that you will encounter through your understanding the principles of the religion you choose to use. No truth is finite to the incarnate. See how the history of that religion shows the corruption introducing laws that are evidently controlling the disciples and the way they conduct their lives. This corruption then spreads through a community and into the populace. In the history of Christianity, you will find that theory has been replaced by fact and the myths have become historical. The truth of the foundation of Christian belief is fiction and the fiction is now the truth.

Spirit intends that spirituality will replace religion. The difficulty is in allowing unrestricted growth of spirituality in a society that depends on control and order that is determined by the members of that society. We suggest that the best-structured religion is the Christian religion. It does need the controls removed. The words of Jesus clearly indicate that God consciousness is what he endeavoured to teach. His followers then made him God and passed all responsibility to Jesus to save them. If you wanted to become one of the followers you had to agree to the rules of the society. These rules were created by certain principles such as Paul and Constantine. One made the religion now called Christianity and the other turned it into political power that he spread throughout his empire in order to control the population. The latter introduced a creed that still exists today as the basis for Christian belief. It does allow you to say that you can know God only believe in Him. Christianity suggests that the only way into heaven is through Jesus and yet we know that there is unlimited access to this world even if you haven't heard of Jesus and even if you lived in your world before Jesus existed. If you heed the words of the teacher Jesus you can get the awareness that heaven exists. You can also see that he speaks of the many levels of consciousness that exist in the Spirit world. He demonstrates the ability you have to heal. He also demonstrates the ability you have to access the truth and the need to share your truth with everybody. He is reported to have said that in his Father's house there are many mansions – this refers to the existence of heaven and the many levels of consciousness. He has said that you must heal the sick and preach the kingdom. This can only mean that through your mutual interdependency you can heal each other through the spiritual aspects of your awareness and that you need to share your truth.

Remember that in the time of Jesus there was no Christian church. There was no Christian religion. Jesus in appointing Peter his representative could only have been as a result of the trust he placed in him and recognition of his spirituality. Jesus obviously wanted the truth kept simple and indeed true.

Go rest in the knowledge that you are your won saviour, that you have the means and ability to save yourself. All this is part of Creation as ordained by God.

THE NEW PHASE.

The next phase in the development can now begin. The first phase was to draw attention to the fact that Spirit and the Spirit world exist. This recognition is achieved through the revelations of the ability to receive healing from a discarnate source (we refer to spiritual healing and none other): also that there is evidence gained through good spiritually based clairvoyance, clairaudience and clairsentience. There is no way that any evidence of Spirit can be gained unless it is through spiritual practices. If the practice is not called by its proper title then it cannot be expected that Spirit will assist it

This new phase is based upon the fact that more people can claim to be more aware of the nature of Spirit and of their own Spirit. It has happened that humankind has become engrossed in its physical aspects and has ignored its Spirit. Much of the resistance to the philosophy of Spirit is because of the resistance of humankind to release themselves from the ego aspects of their being and to view their life from the spiritual aspects. In the case of the driver of a motorcar it is the driver that determines the direction the vehicle takes, the speed it travels at, and how it is guided around the various obstacles that the car is likely to encounter on its way. The car if left to its own devices cannot be relied upon to take its driver safely to the driver's destination. The body cannot be relied upon to safely take its Spirit to the Spirit's destination. Unfortunately, the body, because of its sensibility, responds to certain stimulations only on a physical level and generally ignores the opinion of the Spirit in its decision-making process. This is where most have difficulty in evolvement. The Spirit comes first and the body comes second. We have spoken about death and have said that it is the Spirit that decides when it has finished with the body. When the Spirit decides that it has fulfilled its purpose it can choose to go home to the Spirit world or to continue to enjoy earth life for a longer period. If the Spirit finds that the body has taken too much control it can decide to take the next available opportunity to leave the body – a minor accident can have fatal consequences. Most illnesses are as a result of the body, through its over controlling of its Spirit, needs the intervention of some physical malady to reduce the power of the body and thus enable the Spirit resume control and avoid the desperate measures referred to above. The guidance we have imparted to you is to be applied to the spiritual understanding that you have. The awareness this will give you will help you transform your life in such a way that you will see life differently. This in turn will bring certain complications in that friends and associates will see things differently to you and this will cause them to worry about you and your view of life. This should not be a reason for you to revert to the way you were. If you seek to revert you will find that you will never be satisfied as a dimension of understanding has been lost and you miss it. Once you have discovered the dimension of Spirit in your life there should be no need for anything else. Life will become complete and all should go well in your development. People will be unnerved by your completeness. They will want what you have but will have to face the same letting go that you had to do. They will have to take their own road just as you had to find and take yours. The only advantage they will have is, should they remain your friend they will have you to reassure them that they are on the right path. You who read these words are going through a different process. You have chosen to encounter these words and to act upon them. This will lead to your development. If you save these words you have them to reassure you. If you partake in a meditation group then you will find friends who are in the same situation as you are and that too can be reassuring for you.

You are well into the second phase if you still read and use the power of these words, we give you.

Rest awhile and savour these words we give to you. Go with God's Love.

RELIGION.

Like Jesus, we do not come to you to create a new religion. Our purpose is to help you, humankind, evolve. Your purpose is to continue evolving so that eventually you will re-merge with God. Religion is not the way. The way is through spiritual awareness and that is what we seek to help you find. It is not enough for you to comply with the rules of your chosen religion. Use your religion to help you understand the way of Spirit and apply this to the understanding of your life purpose. See if your religion helps you do this.

We have said that spirituality is the basis of all religions. Religions unfortunately have lost the idea of spirituality and preferred to use the term spiritual in order to legitimise their true purpose. What is the true purpose of religions? We see it as to have power. Humankind thirsts for power. We see this all the time. It is difficult for us to compete when all we can offer to humankind is the knowledge that they have all the power they need, and do not need to seek more.

It was this seeking of power that got you into trouble in the first place. In the beginning there was God entirely. God is a composition of energies. Each energy has a special function in God. A physical body is a composition of cells. Each cell has a special function in the body. In God we will call these energies individual Spirits. These individual Spirits are you the Spirit, and us the Spirit. Each individual Spirit is composed of many essences. Each essence has a special function in the Spirit. For a body cell to malfunction creates disease. For an essence to malfunction creates disharmony. For an individual Spirit to malfunction creates the situation you find yourself in. When a human cell runs amuck you can find, for example that cancer has taken hold of the body. When part of God sought to be the power, rather than an integral part of the power, that part alienated itself from God. It experienced its own ignorance. In order to reunite with God that part has to educate itself to its own power and function. This is what you, and also we, are about.

We have already said that no one is more evolved than another. We have also said that all are evolved differently. We here are evolved differently than you. It is that difference that helps us help you and the application of your experiences to our lives helps us. We are all on the path back to God. Where we talk of the different components malfunctioning it is only to put the situation into understandable terms. It is a difficult concept to communicate to you, as your reality cannot offer a better description. In general, it is how we have said but there is more to it. To learn more about this occurrence will not help you in your present state. It is sufficient to say that creation was the answer to your needs so that you had only to follow life as presented to you and you will find your way home to God.

You have been shown that creation is perfect and that there is no right or wrong as such. There is the way that takes you forward and there is the way that takes you nowhere. It is as simple as that. There is no need for self-punishment as punishment happens automatically. The law of cause and effect is very complete and if you understand this law you will see that by following it you will find the way. Good or bad experiences are the result of this law operating in your life. Good work takes you onward and bad work allows you no progress. To enjoy life indicates that you are experiencing fulfilment. If you are fulfilled you experience satisfaction and have no demands. If you have no demands you can progress to your next experience. When we say that you have no demands it does not mean that you cease all movement forward. Without demands you can move forward lighter and with direction. You will not know the direction until you take it and it feels enjoyable if its right. You will not know where you are going until you get there and you are happy if its right. Creation in its perfection offers you the opportunity of making a decision based on what your life is presenting to you. What your life is presenting to you has been created for you by the law of cause and effect which in turn is working in accordance with the input you have made by the actions you have just committed. Always know that God loves you.

Always know that God has not left you powerless in your life. Always know that there is no task set for you that you cannot master. Always know that God awaits you. Always know that there is a place for you in God.

MISCONCEPTIONS.

We see that you enjoyed our last words. There are many other misconceptions that are entertained by humankind. These misconceptions are not restricted to any particular culture or part of your earth. They are not restricted to any belief system. This frame of mind occurs when ignorance is replaced by a need for that vacant space to be filled with any "reason" for any reason. In other words when the truth is unacceptable there is still a void that seeks fulfilment and that then is a vulnerable space in the thinking of humankind. The person who seeks a "truth" that satisfies them often draws a lie to them. The truth will tell you that you have much to learn whereas this type of lie tells you that you know it all already. We have spoken of knowledge and how you possess all knowledge, but in a way that impedes its usage in a positive way. By this we mean that knowledge needs wisdom with it in order for it to be safe to use.

Take for example playing with fire. It is easy for you to light a fire. You know that a fire has the potential to burn. Even though you know these facts, how many times have you burnt yourself? The more you experience the burns the wiser you become and the safer it is for you to use fire. The more you use fire the more you discover how useful fire is – and this knowledge existed and you then repeat your experiments with the usage of fire and become wiser still – and safer. So, you can see that to educate you to your knowledge is not enough but you must also have the opportunity to discover the application of that knowledge in order to generate the wisdom to make it safe to know so much. Those individual Spirits that we spoke of when they were part of God lacked the wisdom and the knowledge of the power they had. This is why in your incarnate state you are wiser after the event – always.

There is a very important point that we wish to make at this stage. Humankind often wonders why they have to suffer so much. We have explained to you how it is that the resistance to the truth often needs trauma to be applied to it in order that the human being takes notice. Watch other animals and how they approach a situation in their lives. Watch the dog as he approaches a situation that might present danger. He will continue on his chosen course but with a greater alertness constantly ready to react to any change in the situation. He will continue to sniff his way forward and at the slightest threat will immediately take evasive action and thus avoid grief. As he resumes his journey, he does not hesitate in order to analyse the situation rather he takes the options presented to him by the circumstances that prevail. A human act's differently. A human ventures forward full of courage and often blind resolve. They have a goal and the single-minded intention of achieving it – no matter what happens. When a human encounters a situation that suggests that there will be trouble, he/she squares their shoulders and continues forward even if it means battle. This is the ego again causing the human to be blind to the course of action they need to take. The law of cause and effect also plays a part in the consequences of this misplaced determination. The human goes wilfully into to danger and thus must suffer the consequences of that decision. We used the word suffer because that is most often the consequences of blind determination. Most ships are lost at sea because of blind determination. If you fight nature you are destined to fail. If you work with nature you will not fail and often will succeed – provided you allow that to survive any experience is always a success, and the degree to which you survive makes you successful.

The blindness that causes you to suffer most often can only be caused by ignorance. How many healers think that by calling their therapy spiritual that it is spiritual healing? If they were true spiritual healers, they would not call their therapy any other name nor would they make great claims around the effectiveness of the therapy. There is a difference in recounting instances of healing that the healer has experienced and making claims, but spiritual healing can stand on its own merits by producing the correct results. Spiritual healing is consistent as Spirit is consistent. spiritual anything is consistent. This is why many try to endorse their efforts by suggesting that it is spiritual and this would include religions. Spiritual is of the Spirit and if this is not truly the case then it is not spiritual no matter how it might be named.

Somebody claims to heal through the power of Jesus. Jesus, the body, is dead. The Spirit who chose that body called Jesus is again incarnate. Where then does this healing come from? Does it come from the now powerless remains of the body or does it come from the power that was in that body? We can tell you that there is no power of Jesus. You can receive a power but from a discarnate being that likes to impersonate the great ones in order to feed the ego that they still attach themselves to. This ego is often that of the healer we have just described. Spiritual healing requires a clear channel for Spirit to work through. It is the knowledge of Spirit that the healer has that allows this channel. The more aware the healer is of this knowledge the greater the channel. The greater the spiritual wisdom the safer the channel is for the healer and the safer the healing is for the one who seeks healing through that channel

It is that time for rest now. Digest these words at your leisure. There is no urgency. There is no need to be misled. There is no need for you to feel you should suffer in order to advance in life. God awareness is your only need. If you have that, all else will be simple.

God blesses you with life.

BLIND FAITH.

Dear friends we come in a joyous mood this time. We have for many weeks been attempting to pass to you the awareness of the knowledge that you possess. Many of you have reacted to this information and many have acted on it. Those who have reacted must indeed examine their reaction.

We have stated before that we do not come to teach you a new religion, or to judge you, or to condemn you. We have said that you have no need to fear us or to feel that you have to radically change your ways lest you find hell. We have not said that you must denounce all existing beliefs nor to blindly follow our tuition. We have not imposed any condition upon you that should cause you to feel the need to react. We have sought to cause you to think, to examine the many hypotheses that you hold as truths, to question the subject of power, to become aware of the controls in your life. If on the other hand you were to act upon the information we have passed to you, then you will by now have felt the change that is taking place in your life as the hypothesis becomes the truth or that you have de-powered that hypothesis until the time occurs when you can find the truth that it holds for you. This truth is simply that the hypothesis was correct or equally that it was incorrect. If it is correct then you can act upon it and if it is proven that it is incorrect you can discard it. The information we have given to you suggests that you must not act on blind faith. Therefore, we do not wish that you should accept all that we say in blind faith but to keep this information as a hypothesis until it either becomes true for you or else disregard what has been said. We have said that time is the greatest tool to use in seeking truth as truth is always waiting to be discovered and that can take time. You therefore can leave the hypothesis at the back of your consciousness until some event in your life triggers your memory of it and you can then apply the hypothesis and decide that it is true or not. If it is true then you can act upon it. On the other hand, if you have already reacted to our words the truth lies buried under the misinformation that you possess and that has caused you to react. You then proceed through life entrenched in your fixed mind unaware of the truth or lies that are guiding or controlling you. This is a sorry state for anybody to be in especially as the truth is there waiting to be found.

We started this dissertation saying we are in a joyous mood. This is so that we can share with you the good feelings that are to be had. We realise that there are many who read these words that have, and will, take them to heart. This gladdens us. Those who enjoy and act upon these words will enjoy the truth so much that they will hunger for more and will also proclaim their truth to others, thus spreading the word. In this way those who rejected the words initially will eventually re-encounter them and get another opportunity to consider them. Again, we refer to time and truth being there for all to use. "If you don't believe us wait and see." You are aware of this expression?

These words are given in love. There is no suggestion that if you do not heed them that there will be repercussions for you. There is nowhere for these repercussions to come from. It is you who have time, but realise that that time is also coupled to sequence when it is addressed in spiritual terms. We have told you that we have no time but that the law of cause and effect shows that there is always a sequence of events that marks the progress of development. It is difficult to see this when you are so controlled by the 24hr clock. You have many sayings about time that fits better to sequential time rather than hour, minutes or days. "There is no time like the present." "Everything in its own time", "When the time is right", and lots more. No saying refers to an hour, day, or year but suggests that time has a place where a particular event can happen more appropriately.

Time beckons us. It is time for us to take our leave for now. We leave you in God's blessed hands. Go in Love.

BELIEF AND TRUTH.

It is often said that there is no surprise without rational explanation. The surprise expressed by those who find that the beliefs they have held as true and yet were not true can also be rationally explained. The degree of surprise is directly proportional to the degree that the believer held belief as being the truth and multiplied by the degree the believer was expressing blind faith in that belief. We are surprised they are surprised as it is more rational that truth is discovered as it is there. Belief is a state and truth is a fact.

This latter is but one of many questions we see being raised around these writings. It is a great disappointment for many people to realise their insignificance in the world. Many have spoken of humankind being a greater species than animal and yet the human is an animal. Many have said that of all animals, mankind is superior but ask yourself how many wars have any other animal started. Look how humankind fight for supremacy and destroy so much goodness. Look how the cat sleeps peacefully by the fire, how faithful a dog is as a companion. Listen to how sweetly the birds sing, how prettily the butterfly looks, how useful the cow is, how powerful the horse is, how necessary the spider is. We could go on. Now look at humankind. Ask yourself how you compare to the other animals that share your planet with you. Are you worthy as a human being to stand on an equal platform with any of those we have spoken of? We see you differently. You argue, resist the truth in case it might destabilise your already shaky life. Other animals are more understanding of the role they play in creation and therefore cause much less problems for all kind. Mankind thinks it is their duty to step on everything in order to reach the top. Other animals do not abuse each other as humankind does. Look to other animals to see the rules of good behaviour. Learn some of these rules and maybe you will find that your life can be somewhat more comfortable and fulfilling.

We have said to you before that your life is one of interdependency. Interdependency extends throughout your world. Every part of creation plays an important role in this interdependency. No one thing is of lesser or greater importance. The world cannot exist as it is unless everything that exists in it is currently playing that role. Mankind unbalances that fine balance created by God. All animals depend on life being as it should be with the only change required being dictated by evolution. Animals, other than the human species, do not invent new goods and then mass produce them and market them. This is a trait of humankind. This trait often leads to great problems that directly affect you environment. Other animals suffer the consequences of the human animals meddling in the role of creator. Look at how your world is being threatened by the many unhealthy industries that are polluting the atmosphere of your planet. Many of these same industries pollute the very basic elements such as water. Humankind is composed of a high percentage of water and yet humankind fails to see how it is destroying itself albeit that it is a slow process.

Humankind is not this great species that it thinks it is. Just because no other animal breeds other animals for food does not mean the other animals are stupid. Just because no other animal keeps a human or other animal as a pet does not mean that they are a subspecies. Just because no other animal trains a human to behave, go fetch, protect or some other trick is only because humankind in its arrogance does not realise that indeed other animals do just that. Do you have a pet? How does it affect your life? Can you just go away on holidays without making plans to have your pet looked after? Who opens the cans of food for your pet? Who provides a warm place for them to sleep in? Who's the pet and who's the master? Who's the fool?

Go with God's Love and take your place amongst all animals doing what comes naturally for you – but with rational.

NEEDS AND WANTS (1).

One cannot always be or feel that which they want to be. Achievement can only be gained after first studying ones role in this life. We can all entertain all sorts of desires, all sorts of wants, but these are of no merit without understanding ones real needs.

The separation of our needs from our wants is the first role we need to study. We have often spoken of this subject, and again we must look at it again, in fact we must regularly question our motives in this regard. People often come seeking development because they want to be like some of the better-known mediums. The question is why? Is this just ego? Generally, it is. To these people it must be said that the path they thread is one to disillusion and destruction; destruction to others by misguidance; destruction to themselves by drawing away from their purpose, and very often damaging their body, and again damaging their mind. Those who seek to develop their psychic abilities generally want only the results and care neither the source nor the cost.

The path to God is not along one motivated by ego; the path to God is not along the one motivated by selfish desire; the path to God is not along the one motivated by fear; and the path to God is not along one motivated by insecurity. No my friend, the path to God is along one motivated by needs, the need to get to God, the need to be of help to others seeking the same goal, the need to be of service to those powers of Spirit that seek to help mankind in this need, and by carrying God's torch into the darkness in the name of the divine light, to illuminate the pathways for those who also have a need to return home. Yes friends, the path to God is along unselfish ways, with no wants only the need to be or have whatever is necessary to get there and no more. Naturally whatever tools are needed will be provided, yes, and the overalls also, for this is a job of work, a life's work. It is work for a good master and is a difficult task, sometimes even dirty. Do not fear as all the necessary precautions will be taken. Have trust.

Go with God's Blessings.

THE CENTRE.

Friends it is with a little precaution that I approach you this night for we see that all are not in the mind that is necessary to receive Spirit in the correct manner. Too many still seek for the spectacular manifestation of Spirit and not the more subtle manner of teaching. It is in the latter practice that we excel, though we have been known to produce performances of a psychic nature in the past. It is not our intention that these performances should be repeated in the same way as before. We do promise however that those who do follow the path to Spirit will not be disappointed in the performances that will take place in their life.

We see many who wait to come to this Centre but who do not. This delay is mainly due to two reasons; firstly, that this Centre has and is being misrepresented by some who attend it and secondly by those who attend not being open to inform others. In the first instance those attending need to carefully examine their true reasons for attending. Is it because they were informed by some psychic that they had abilities of a psychic nature? Is it because they feel it would be nice to attend a mysterious organisation dealing in matters occult? Is it that the Centre would provide them with the necessary information to set up a similar movement with a view that they may become an important person and make lots of money? If anyone should now entertain any notion of any of these ideas then they would be advised that they are in the wrong place and had best heed this advice - this is not your place unless you want to change. If one does not find themselves in this foregoing category, then examine the other category, that of being secretive. There is no reason why one should feel that the message of the Centre is only for them. No, the message of the Centre is of a universal, all denominational nature. Why should one deny that they are seeking God, that they are seeking themselves, that they are seeking the truth about life? There is no reason, is there? Well then maybe those who find this cap fitting will break the barriers that bind them and feel free to help others around them in a more positive way.

Lastly, we would like to tell all who listen to this message that the only person who would be fooled by this stupidity is one's own self. We in Spirit know what it is that lies within a body and the motivation that is in operation; we are not fooled by words or outward appearances. No friends, do not be so naive to think that. It is the task of all to find their own truths, to be honest with themselves, and to be honest with others. Don't forget the only fool in the end will be oneself.

It is with these thoughts that we leave you this night, we also ask that God will leave you with His blessings and that He will provide you with the wisdom and knowledge to untangle yourselves from the web that has been so deftly spun around you.

God blesses you all.

TRUST IN SPIRIT.

(At a time when many people were suggesting that the teachings were not reliable and sought to undermine the work of the Irish Spiritual Centre, Spirit sent these inspiring and reassuring words. Brendan.)

My friend heed not the words of others who do not sign that declaration, that complete trust in the guidance is the key to uninterrupted communication from your friends in Spirit. This I say so that you can only know that what you are receiving is of the truest nature and comes only from the light. You sit this night to receive what is generally referred to as knowledge or teachings. I do not like to disappoint you but in this instance, I feel that I must for in all fairness to you it is felt that your mind must feel overtaxed by the trivia of every day, day to day living. Listen to what I say, it is a preoccupation with the mundane that prohibits your development and what best way to divert your attention than to call out for the assistance you are always so ready to provide. My friend you have once again been used, you have been accused of not having the same compassion that you have had, this cannot be so or else you would not have responded to the call you received, would you. Examine yourself not. The future work will necessitate a greater degree of separation in the physical sense but will also require a greater bond of togetherness in the spiritual way. There is so much work to be done that one cannot sufficiently or efficiently carry out the necessary work, it is the work of many, too much time is being devoted to those who in reality do not need the attention they demand therefore be cautious of those selfish seekers.

And now we will talk of the work in hand. Yes it will be nice when finally you settle into the additional room, but it is not the most urgent situation we see needing to be done. The welfare of those attending the Centre is of the greatest priority. We have spent much time organising a group that has strength yet they will not co-operate with Spirit. There are plenty who will take up the task of teaching but they would rather play the dumb ignorant fool. We see these with a degree of displeasure though it is their will that they exercise and this is sacred to them. It is their divine right that they use.

We talk tonight of further frailties that present themselves, the interaction of numerable types on one core. It is only by the utmost tolerance and understanding that any cohesion can exist. It is of paramount importance that all learn that it is not of the individual to strive ahead into the obscure future unprepared and alone, a hero. No, it must be realised that the relinquishing of the will to the work of Spirit is to enlist in an army, all fighting to achieve the same goal, God. When this is understood then perhaps the greater message can be given and understood. This message contains the understanding that when this army marches it is to a definite plan and not a haphazard excursion. The divine plan that unfolds will show that everything has been carefully thought out and can only be implemented by the selfless giving of the life to the work in hand, the work of God.

When on this true path there is no time for trips of fancy into fairy tale worlds, too much time has already been spent at doing this already. The work of God must be treated as seriously as the desire to be by his side, and even more seriously to be part of the Godhead. My friend there is much that needs discussion. There is much that needs to be seen. Too many seek to cloud your vision, as before those who were of selfish ways sought to allow you only to see that which they were prepared to show you, now we will see to it that you will all that is to be seen. We will come another night with the universal message for the people in the Centre so that they to may learn the knowledge and the wisdom that is to be theirs.

May God offer you all blessings and may you see fit to receive them. You have our love.

SELF-EXAMINATION.

My friends it is of utmost importance this day that we continue our examination of our motivations. Most will judge from a self-righteous way that they are aware that their motivation is correct and therefore refuse to continuously examine themselves. It so happens that nobody can afford to adopt this attitude, as this is only the opening into the pit that awaits them. When one feels they have the right path chosen it would be illogical to accept that they have the ultimate answer, they have not. On every path there are many levels, each level with a teacher of particular abilities.

How would it be possible for anybody to progress if they do not recognise this and allow this change to take place? They must be prepared to accept change. Many feel that the ultimate goal is to get to God, it is. How many are aware that the God they seek may not be the God that they need? An illustration of this is the typical situation where one feels that they will first do a period of living and then they will spend time looking for that "elusive" God. That person has no concept of the role that they have taken up. They have put another goal before God, a goal that to them is, at that moment in time, their God. There is no way that this person can expect to ever achieve their true destination. You see the simple ways that we can mislead ourselves.

The real nature of truth is simplicity, but because of the complications of humanity and the lack of simple comprehension the message gets lost. We in Spirit do not find such difficulty as this because we find no need to be intellectual or in any way to be other than as we are. This to you may appear simplistic, however we would suggest you read again the words as given before and how you saw them apply to yourself. They were written for you all, there is no need to feel that you were not to be included in what was said. Even if they do not appear to fit be aware that there is still time for that to happen. No one in the flesh can ever say they have the total answer, nor can they say they have got beyond temptation; nor can they say that they are exempt from any of the teachings of Spirit. If anyone were this evolved then there would be no necessity for Spirit to devote so much to the enlightenment and upliftment of the human race.

It invariably happens that a little knowledge is allowed to go a long way, usually too long. The essence of good communication with the world of Spirit is to first define your need in relation to this. This is very important as you can only get that which you seek. You have often heard the expression that like attracts like, rather this should read like seeks like. The same applies to calling on God, you first have to define which God it is that you seek. There are many Gods created by mankind, the god of money, the god of power, the god of destruction, the god of cruelty. There are many gods created by mankind, each with a special purpose to suit the selfish wants of the idolater. Any time that you put anything in front of God, you by your own right, denounce the truth of the living God, the Supreme Spirit whom we all love, respect and seek. Put the one true God as your goal; see all else as being secondary to this goal. Yes, go and enjoy life, but in a real manner, in a spiritual manner and then you will find that life takes on a better complexion, a happier tone, a higher vibration. Then you will be in a better position to achieve the goal you should so desire.

With these thoughts I leave you now. I hope that I may have enlightened you somewhat to the story of living and that I have in no way left you confused. I leave you now in the hands of my Father God that He may be visible to you as your goal. May He give you His blessing of Understanding.

TESTING TIMES.

(At this time in the Irish Spiritual Centre there was a difficulty with motivating the people attending to assist in carrying out the work of the Centre. Spirit had the following comments to make. It is also interesting to note that at this stage in the current writings Spirit saw the same situation arising in the Centre and that these words were appropriate. This also illustrates the awareness and interest that Spirit has in the work of the Centre. Brendan)

My friend, we speak of more mundane matters and leave the matter of teaching to the time which is right. We speak tonight of the function of the centre.

As you are aware the onus for the welfare of those attending the centre has again been placed at your feet. Many times you have striven to encourage others to share this responsibility but they were not capable of meeting this challenge. Yes, it is a challenge for them, at stake is a test of their true sincerity and honesty. If they find that it is not within their capabilities then they must be the first to admit it and seek instead to reform themselves and try to attain the degree of evolvement that is necessary to take the task. Many have thought that they were of the calibre to do the work or at least the work that they thought needed to be done, very often the work they saw was as they would like to see themselves working. This type of behaviour we do not pander to. Those have been guided from the role they saw themselves play towards the role that really needs to be carried out. The great test they now face is will they be prepared to stay within the guidance or will they feel that their place is not within the Centre. We will see, as they have their free will, we cannot prejudge their decision. We can only await the outcome.

And now on other matters, we see that A. is not really taking the task presented to them seriously enough and yet they do treat the situation with too much seriousness. They will find it difficult to understand what we are referring to but they must understand that we do not reproach them. We find that the delay in making a full decision to do the necessary work in the centre has put a delay on all advancement. They must not dither any longer. The teachings that have been given for the meditation nights are truly for them to read, and through this reading they will get the necessary impetus to engender their own unique form that is yet to be established between their friends and themselves. This is a very major role for them to play and one that they are quite capable of handling. their hesitancy is totally understood by us, we also realise that if you were to ask then they may protest but will not refuse. You chose them carefully; it just took time for us to manoeuvre them and you into the right positions and with adequate knowledge to lead the army that has to be formed.

You see that you too were unaware of the plan that had been made. There are as yet many, many who have yet to come and as they arrive, they too will not be aware of the plan that they are part of. It will be difficult to sustain their interest for too long a time, it will be preferable that they will be carefully watched for and when discovered, to keep their interest in the Centre. They will not be very strong as their journey has been very arduous. They will not even know why they have arrived at the Centre, let alone to what degree their involvement will be. You can only be aware of these people should you be in a position to meet them before they get carried away down the path of others and miss their path entirely.

This task of discovery cannot be tackled from behind a desk. The desk presents a formidable obstacle for those new people who will enter. We have sent many to you with the capabilities of very fine leadership yet they have shown a reluctance to get too involved in this respect of the centre. It is time now for these to start to practice more of the teachings that they have received. This is a task you must address yourself to as soon as possible, look for the release from the more mundane duties of the Centre, leave those jobs to those who are best equipped to handle them. They must be allowed to see their tasks and be persuaded to carry them out. You may help but they must do.

I leave you this night with these thoughts and an earnest request that the Father may delegate sufficient strength to assist you in these endeavours in His name. I leave you my love as I have received yours on many occasions. God blesses you.

GREATER TEACHINGS.

It is with apprehension that I approach you this night. There is a reason for this, for already I feel that people have taken exception to the words that I have given. It is impossible to stress sufficiently that the words given are not to be taken as a reproach, no, they are to be taken as a lesson to help in the understanding of Spirit, your Spirit, and the purpose of your existence on the earth.

That existence is often mistaken as punishment for some form of wrong doing, it is not. The fact that somewhere in the distant past the Spirit that is within you transpired to usurp the authority of God, leading to its downfall into the abyss, is of no concern to the 'you' of to-day. No, the 'you' of to-day has to concern itself with the immediate task in hand, that of returning to the grace in God. It is not a punishment; it is in fact a reward for having the sight to see that the Light exists, a reward for wanting to return to that Light. Wallow not in self-pity; rather rejoice for you are on your path.

Now I say we may speak of brighter matters. It is to be that facilities are to be made for greater teachings, but first we must be sure that all minds are attuned sufficiently to receive and understand what is to be given. It is not a question of great intellect, rather an ability to understand simplicity itself. The world has so complicated the minds of mankind with the deviousness of the very devil itself that it has by doing so blinded the eyes, deafened the ears and gagged the mouths, not so they should not utter evil, nor see evil, nor hear evil, rather that the Light could not be countenanced.

This time is just one of many where the teachings of Spirit are to be given to this Centre, and through this Centre to those who are outside. There is no estimating how far these words will reach. There is even a lesson to be gained by this latter statement, and that is, that it is up to you who listen now, to carry these words into your life with you, for these are the words of Spirit, Spirit who works for God, Spirit who seeks to help humankind in the name of God. These are therefore the words of God, like God they are endless. Though the message is simple the way is difficult. There are many questions to be asked by many people, each deserving an adequate answer. How can it be possible to cover all, if it is not for the many people who are aware of Spirit, helping in their own way to help God and consequently other people who flounder in the morass called living in the "real" world. This is the real world, a world of Light, peace, love and harmony. What better a place to be. On an individual level, it would be impossible to reach all with the simple words that are used, it can only be as a generalisation that any impart can be made. Provision will be made in the future for private sittings on a more intimate scale for those more serious seekers, but first we seek that the understanding is sufficient to be able to make decisions for oneself and know that they can be honoured.

Many times in the past, people who have attended this Centre have made pacts, commitments, but only in so far that they could benefit for personal selfish reasons. These people have gone their own ways, they have not brought Spirit from the Light with them. If this is so what have they brought with them? That is the important question. Now you know why it was that we started this communication as we did. We asked that you examine your own motivation in such a way that you had no question regarding your desires to come to this Centre to take this path. There are no sworn pacts to be made, no sworn agreements, no it is up to you as yourself to decide which direction and to where it is you want to go, free will. We do not demand anything from you but we do ask that you understand your reasons for being here.

I feel that this is sufficient for this time, therefore, I pray that God may bestow upon you His peace and love and that your meditation may give you a further glimpse into the bright future that awaits you should you decide to go and seek it. You all have my love and the love of those who guide you. Go in peace and understanding.

God blesses you all.

THE SPIRAL OF GREED.

It is with peace in mind that I come to you. These previous few times that we have been together have been testing trying times but like any good foundation it has to be allowed to settle first and after a period of curing can then be built upon. This night shall be spent in examining the question of orthodox teachings on Spirit.

In early times all was reasonably well in the world you inhabit, man trusted man within reason, and a certain sense of serenity prevailed allowing the various tasks that each had to perform to be accomplished. Then came the advantage taker, he grabbed what he could with the minimum of effort. This human lived a world of no spiritual advantage. Those who suffered at the hands of this human resolved not to be fooled again in such a manner. They watched the wrongdoer and saw only the superficial signs of well-being, a surplus of material goods piled around his door. Jealousy began to manifest and soon all wanted those goods back and as the original wrongdoer was too smart and watched his back too well, they had to find another easier source. Thus began the spiral of greed, the gaining of material wealth at the least by the easiest method and at the most at any cost. Many are the stories that have been told of the man who sells his very soul so that he may gain material wealth.

So to, when it came to spiritual matters there were those who sought this method to gain not only material wealth by usurping spiritual power but also sought to control others by overshadowing them with the darkness that would follow such a trial, keeping as many as possible ignorant of the real spiritual truths. All to many used this form of corruption to control the masses. So as this ignorance could be maintained power structures were formed so that many more could be controlled. Many of these larger units were eventually to become the foundations for early orthodox religions. We are aware that many here this time will throw up their hands in horror at the suggestion that their religion may be included in a group such as this, yet we pray that they will bear with us a little further so as we may fully enlighten them. One simple question, why, if the teachings were kept pure was it necessary for so many in Spirit to be asked to attend the human race and tell them the truth? Do you have a simple answer?

Look back into the humankind history, see all those that you call prophets that have attended, each carrying the same message, that the truth has been misrepresented. Their teachings have been similar and have been similarly corrupted. Even now look at the divisions that exist within Christianity, they are many. How can this be so if they are solely truths? Man has a consistency, that is, portraying the truth as best befits him. We here in Spirit remind you of this for it is knowledge that you are familiar with in your Spirit role. Why else would you be there if it were not for the opportunity to learn what real truth is? Yes, my friends that is one of the reasons why you are on the earth. There is another reason associated with this and that is to then go away, exercise the truth you find so as to implement the return to all truth, the return to God. It is the duty of every human that they shall proclaim this truth to whom-so-ever asks. Now it is known that you find this a difficult task but take notice you are only asked to give to those who ask. Wait until they ask, then tell, then watch. It may take time for this seed to begin to grow but be assured it will.

There will be no need for remorse if at first your statement is refuted, be assured that Spirit is behind the question, the questioner, the answer and you the answerer. There is not much effort in this task. In most areas where Spirit operates, we understand the difficulties that are experienced by humankind; however, we do try and make things as easy as possible. One difficulty we experience with humankind is the lack of trust that they have for Spirit. Spirit has never and would never refuse a sincere request for help, very often the petitioner lacking the trust or patience interferes with the actions of Spirit and the results are disastrous. We have so many times seen human interference and seen the consequences, which have been so bad that no prophet/redeemer could be expected to salvage even the merest portion of spiritual sanity from the mess that is there. It has been at times such as this that the world has had to stop and restart, let's hope there is no repeat of this calamity.

I will take my leave from you now and trust you have not found these words repugnant to your beliefs and that you will see them as they are truly meant, an opening in the curtain of mists that have been woven about the minds of humankind.

I leave you with your own friends in the Spirit world who, should you listen to them, tell you these same truths. Go with all the Blessings of God into your world, stronger for these words.

EPITOME OF MISFORTUNE.

It is the epitome of misfortune to have lived a life and not have moved forward one iota. It is for this reason that we come in such frequency, so as to help define the parameters of the necessary motivation that will take all into the world that is yet to come from this that they now occupy. Again, I refer to the many doubts that previous communications have raised in the minds of those who listened to the words. Again, I stress that the purpose of these communications is to enlighten not to dumbfound.

We have said many times that the purpose is to advance forward to God. This advancement that is for you to make is of benefit to not only you but to many others who watch so that they too may learn and in their way advance towards the Light. Such is the responsibilities that are accepted by you all. I cannot stress sufficiently the importance of the duty you have towards others never mind the duty you have towards yourself. Many have been helped towards the Light in this manner and as they progress the need for the state they exist in continuing decreases.

This also applies to your existence on earth. As you experience that which you need, and benefit positively from it, the need for that experience to continue to exist becomes superfluous. If you can imagine all this achievement on a massive scale, applying to all the Spirits that exist, you can see that somewhere in the future that a certain perfection must be reached and the need for the world as you know it ceases. So too with the successive planes of existence between where you are and the Godhead. As each plane outlives its purpose each alters its state and, with those who used to inhabit that space, moves into the next stage of existence, until finally there is only one stage left with all gathered there collectively with God being known as the ultimate, the Godhead.

I will once again tell you that it is only on attaining perfection that one can be part of that which is perfect, that perfection cannot be attained in one step through this earth because perfection does not exist here. We are all part of imperfection striving to be perfect but realise that it would be folly to try or even think to try and attain the peak while still of this earth. The most that one can strive to do is to arrive at an understanding of the perfection they seek, be open to expanding this understanding and follow the direction of this understanding with the ultimate goal ever present in the consciousness. Thought you may be part of the imperfection you are perfectly formed to develop to the degree of perfection that this lifetime can afford you.

It is hoped that all will persist with this task and that all will help others and consequently themselves towards their goal. This is all I have for you this time.

Go with all God's love, facing the Light. Be aware that you have darkness with you, the shadow that you cast, and understand that if others follow you that you permit them only to share in your darkness. Invite those who enquire about your path to accompany you towards the Light for as long as they feel that this course is applicable to them. When they decide to take their own way do not judge them, allow them this choice. Be concerned only how you make your way.

May God give you all his blessings.

CRIME AND PUNISHMENT.

We will talk again about Cause and Effect. You might see this also as Crime and Punishment though punishment would be the consequence of negative deeds. Remember that positive outcomes are the goal: To partake in some experience and to reap the rewards of the good effects. Things go right when they are done right.

This rule or if you like law applies to everything at all times. Every breath you take, every step you make is subject to this rule. You will recall where we have spoken of responsibility. Responsibility is also an integral part of this law. It does not matter if you understand the rules or not, they will inevitably be applied no matter what and you must be prepared to take responsibility for the outcome.

There can be no excuse. There are no accidents only outcomes. This might appear harsh for us to say but that is the law. Even our writing these words carries a consequence. Whatever way you take them will in some way carry an effect for this writer and this writer has to take responsibilities for writing. You have to take the responsibility for reading them. How you react to these words will also be a responsibility you take on. There can be no going back once you've read them. Do you find these words appear ominous? Why would you feel that? Because perhaps you feel that you have walked into a trap? You might feel that there is no way out. You may feel that you will regret the outcome. You may feel that you will suffer. Why would you have these feeling when in fact these words are to help you develop your awareness into a better understanding of all matters and their relevance to your life. You are not responsible for anyone else.

You indeed are not responsible for anyone else – except that you should take on that responsibility. That again is your choice and subject to the law of cause and effect. How can you possibly understand anyone else's choice to incarnate? You cannot – so how can you assume to take responsibility for them? You must avoid this act of responsibility for if you take responsibility for them you allow them avoid taking responsibility for themselves. Do you also want to accept the responsibility of the potential negative outcome of such a selfish act on your part? They will suffer and you will suffer the effects.

Friends help each other but unfortunately often in an unhelpful way. If you study cause and effect you will need to also study your true selfishness and your sense of responsibility, (see earlier writings). Many enter into a task for friendships sake with negative resignation. You will sometimes feel that the commitment you have made on friendship's behalf becomes a chore just when you seek to implement it. However, you have committed yourself and therefore you must go about the business of completing the task. Your actions become unfriendly and you undertake this chore with a bad heart – but you have committed yourself to this task and have to take on the bad feeling you have and to shoulder the responsibilities that you subjected yourself to. Incidentally this can also be the cause of your becoming ill.

You can now see that the law does not allow you to escape the effect of what you have caused by your apparent generosity, your friendly offer of taking on someone else's experiences. The law instead of being applied to them then gets applied to you. They do not escape either as they are also subject to the law all day every day. They, for example, run the risk of your doing the job your way, which could be the wrong way, and because of the trouble you experience and blame them for, they can lose your friendship. On the other hand, if you were to help them in their task by supporting them in doing the best they can, the law will give a more positive outcome. Your friend will feel greater self-esteem, greater strength and a greater respect for your friendship. Both of you can safely accept responsibility for the outcome in your own right.

This is a law worth studying and understanding along with an understanding of selfishness and responsibility. Though these words are from God we take all responsibility for passing them on to you and we hope you will take full responsibility for reading them.

We pray that God blesses you.

ORTHODOX RELIGIONS.

Friends it is imperative that an understanding is reached on Spirits view on orthodox religions. The first point that must be acknowledged is that there is no such thing as orthodox religion in this (the Spirit) world. There are those, who, when they first arrive here think that they have to behave in a manner religious, but it is not long before they realise that all that type of thinking is for the world they have just left. No, we do not have the burden of conformity, like everything here in Spirit there is a clarity that can only come from the freedom that is all prevalent.

We do not have to conform to the man-made laws of God consciousness, what is here is a clearer view of God. To have God consciousness one has first to have an understanding of God. To accept some of the orthodox teachings on God it would make it impossible to have any God consciousness. God has been presented for so long as a God to fear, and to increase that fear churches have set themselves up as the body of representatives of this terrifying god and used this terror to gain power over humankind. The founders of these religions added, as they saw necessary, other facets that they could see would enhance this image of the terrifying ogre. This activity has not yet ceased though it is certainly diminishing and the power slowly leaves the hands of the power seeker.

Be aware that as this structure weakens there will always be those who will seek to take over the control of humankind. This could perhaps be referred to in your terms the coming of the anti-Christ. Again, be wary of such as these. This manifestation can often be seen on a much smaller scale from time to time. In this place we sit in now (the Centre) many struggles have been fought with those seeking power. Those protagonists fail to realise that the power they struggle against is the power of God not the power of any mortal that may of occasion be representing Spirit therein. One can therefore question the validity of motive in these. Spirit is well aware that even as these words are being uttered that there are those who plot to "overthrow" what they may term the hierarchy of this place, the Centre.

We would ask that these power seekers see the senseless trouble that they cause, that they realise that they only bring to themselves sorrow and remorse. Stop, look on us with love as we look on you with love. Is this the way lovers behave? STOP! At this time, we will say no more on this. Listen to the words; question the words, but most of all question yourselves. Question your own naivety. While there is a tug of war going on very little progress is made in any direction. The words are few this time to allow the disruption to resettle. Some who are here (in the Centre) this time will not be here in these rooms much longer. It is only those who can justifiably say that in their very Spirit they seek to return to God, that will find that they can stay.

These words are hard, and harder to say, yet they have to be said for we have seen much scheming going on. We still wish that you are open to the blessings of the Holy One, God Almighty, and that these blessings are bestowed in abundance upon you all. Remember that this is a message addressed to a few through many. Please God you are not one of these few who seek only the power. That was an old lesson we should have learned.

We leave you now in God's hands. Go in peace.

SPIRITUAL DEVELOPMENT (1).

My friends this time we will examine the consequences of seeking to develop ourselves Spiritually. It is inevitable that one day an occurrence will take place and when you relate it to others you will be confronted with very mixed reactions, from incredulity to total amazement.

It is in the nature of humankind to react more to the effect of an experience on others rather than the effect on the person experiencing. An example of this could be that the writer of these words would seek to impress everybody by the "amazing" content and the writer get diverted from the truth in seeking to impress rather than to give the truth as it is. The truth can appear sometimes "boring" and then again sometimes truly amazing. The writer of these words comes from the Light and is therefore in possession of certain truths and can thus only give what is to be given without any recourse to the reception these words might receive. But then the writer of these words is also Spirit not human. It is hoped that this will clarify the query regarding the origins of these writings.

Now we will talk about receiving these words. Again, we would remind you that these words are given in love and that they are in no way meant to astound or amaze you. These words are not given in this instance to give you a greater understanding of Spirit. These words are given to you so that you will get a greater understanding of yourself and you will thus have a greater relationship with Spirit. It is only by this relationship that you and Spirit can be as one in the first place, and like the seed when it becomes one with the ground starts to grow towards the Light, so too your Spirit can begin to grow towards the Light.

We find that many seek to communicate with Spirit without first taking the necessary steps in preparation of the self for this journey. Too many read of various techniques that will help them to "develop" a method of communication. This course takes them on many a perilous journey until eventually they achieve but only a small portion of the benefit they could have had, had they spent the same time in simple meditation for spiritual growth. There is no great secret of the ancients that will unlock the door into this other dimension; rather there is a subtle step to be taken. That step is but a small one towards the Light. This step though small when taken for the first time will be the hardest step you will ever have to take. Later you will be required to take larger, higher, deeper, more purposeful steps but none that will ever be as difficult. In taking this step you will find that it cannot be taken without the full knowledge of Spirit and only with Spirits help.

We leave you now this time as you prepare for your second step. Yes, you have taken the first, you are observing the words of Spirit which you could not have done had you stayed where you were. Now go on to the second. May the Great Spirit, God Almighty take your hand and guide you along the path that takes you to Him.

Go now in peace in God's Light.

SPIRITUAL DEVELOPMENT (2).

For this time, we shall consider the pitfalls that face those in purposeful search for their own spirituality. Success in this search can breed trouble for the unwary earthbound human. It is all too easy to find that there is a factor of ego involved. To find the right path might encourage an overrun of enthusiastic outbursts in the most inappropriate places.

People will find that others will stand in certain awe of the revelations that have befallen the newly initiated. This newcomer to the knowledge can rightly feel a certain pride in their achievement and yet only a certain pride. If one were to feel nothing then there would be no motivation for further progress. This pride is the most likely pitfall that one will encounter in the first instance. It is not a bad thing to entertain a modicum of ego, for that is what this pride may be called, but it is almost impossible to measure the degree of ego that is being entertained. There is no short way that ego can be controlled other than for one to be in constant watch for this insidious emotion to manifest. The most important action is to be aware.

We will move to another matter that can arise in this evolution we talk about. This is another emotion that exists, and this is love. Love is fundamentally the only emotion recognised by Spirit. We are aware that all emotions exist but only in the reality of the human aspect of the Spirit existence.

Love is a very powerful emotion, it can be used in creation, (not necessarily procreation), it can be used for destruction, and it can be used to bind and again to separate. It is indeed a very powerful emotion. Let us look at how love can affect the spiritual evolvement of the Spirit. Firstly, let us understand that the direct opposite of love is hate as bad is the opposite of good. Now with love exposed through meditative processes we must understand that we also have to contend with hate. As we begin to venture along our path balance must be maintained. Love is a very powerful emotion and of itself provides its own protection, however that does not take into account the human factor armed as it is with the fragile free will. This free will can quickly transform love into hate. Again, let us be aware of this, love can quickly transform into hate. It is very important that this is understood because the knowledge of the use of love and the power this emotion contains if used in hate can then become the destructive emotion that not only destroys love but also the user of the hate emotion. Again, be aware of this. This is difficult to speak of, as it is so alien to us here in Spirit, nonetheless we do see the ravages of this emotion. So be aware of these two pitfalls that we have highlighted this time for it is only by awareness that these can be avoided.

These subjects will be examined more at another time but first we will wait and see how you respond to these guidelines.

You see this is caution on our part for the misuse of this knowledge leads only to man's destruction as we witness every day. We seek to educate you away from this destruction not towards it. Go now in the love and light that is good and is the manifestation of God, total and complete. I leave you with these thoughts and all our love also.

SPIRITUAL DEVELOPMENT (3).

My friends it is important that we realise that the reason for the message being given by Spirit is heard by all possible is so that more immediate attention can be given to the evolvement of the Spirit occupying the bodies in the earth environment. It has been a long time since many people realised this and sought the necessary medium so as to be able to contact Spirit themselves. The irony of this is that now Spirit is treated with suspicion by those who encounter it.

There have been many traps laid by the usurpers of the Spirit teachings of old. Nowadays, those who hold these truths are considered outcasts by the very society that seeks to develop an understanding of Spirit, is it because the need to understand is for those other reasons we spoke of before—power and ego? This brings us to the emotion of power, that other insidious emotion. Yes we speak now of power as an emotion, have you never felt power? You have, and it can be addictive also. You seek not to share, keep your little secrets, and pretend that there is really nothing to be discovered. Yes, all are guilty of this in some way or the other. How many have left this place of tuition because this lust for power has not been entertained? The answer to this is that many have. The sad thing about this type of exit is that the power seekers, because of this seeking, cannot leave empty handed and always seek to place the cause of their leaving far from the real truth, usually though they do leave a little clue, notice ego, that place of learning was not good enough for them. They entice others to leave with them. Those who leave for this reason then place themselves further from Spirit, that is Spirit who comes from the Light.

There are many here who await these people and are prepared to pander to their petty need but only as long as is necessary, then the price has to be paid. We shall now emphasise that these words do come from the Light and are only conveyed by me at the express request of God the Creator of all that is perfect. There is a reason that these words must be said, as this place of Spirit teaching has come to the stage in its foundation when it becomes obvious that it is firmly placed in your world. We would again stress that the nature of the "Centre" is there to provide a gathering place for those who are about their purpose in the name of God. It is the purpose of this Centre to help enable humankind to understand the position of its Spiritual evolvement. It is also the purpose of this place to provide a basis for this understanding. It therefore shows that those who seek more without this basic awareness do not realise that there are seeking without foundation. You will notice of late there have been some who have left the Centre, because they didn't find that which they sought. But what was this elusive "thing" that they sought? Was it that which we have outlined before, a power to usurp through ignorance, an ignorance that they failed to recognise and remove through careful study of the simple philosophy of Spirit, the simple truth that all humankind is engaged in the task of returning to God? Where then is there any need to develop power, power of trance, power of mediumship? These abilities are not powers, they are tools for receiving Spirit but must only be used for the benefit of Spirit to help humankind, not for humankind to contact the dead.

There is more to this, that you must realise, but this we will leave until another time. You have much to understand in what has been given this time. Be assured that this is knowledge and has not been given as a direct reflection on any one person. We leave you now in God's care and earnestly pray that this we speak of does not befall you. Go now in God's Light immersed in his Love cosseted from the darkness and coldness of negativity. God blesses you.

NEW PHILOSOPHY.

It is this time that I come to tell you of other things. Though there is only one name given you must realise that there are many communicators at work on each occasion that we communicate. The reason why only one name is given is that the words come from the collective essence, rather like a joint statement but coming from the one source.

We see that you comprehend what it is that we try to say to you. This is good, for you have attuned yourself sufficiently to leave no obstruction in the way. There are times about that cause you concern but you must not let the petty details affect you. There are many who need to know that the strength of the Centre is such that it does not seek numbers to attend for that is not its function. The main function is, as you are aware, to provide for those who need that which you have to give but only as they become aware that they have the need. We cannot convince somebody of the need to ask a question if they do not have the fundamental sensitivity to receive the prompting, we have to give them. We will rest on this matter now; it is sufficient that those who do come for the right reasons get that which they need.

This is the season of new beginnings and I relish the opportunity of being in on the start of this one. Of course, I have participated before with you in other beginnings but never one quite such as this. Magic is being worked and worked well for is not the work of God magic! This I tell you for you must be prepared for many startling happenings that will take place as a result of this beginning. We in Spirit are all prepared for what will take place in the coming period. No, we do not stipulate time but can say this that is about to begin has the full blessing of Almighty God.

The season of spring is upon us, many a fresh growing has started, and some have even flowered. This is the season of freshness and a time to extend the light of day. See like the daylight the spread of the God Light; see how the word of the Spirit has spread; though many have endeavoured to stifle it. You will find that in this writing the theme is on hope, a hope that the word will be spread, a hope that all who read it will benefit. Do not forget it is not a new philosophy that we carry, no the philosophy we carry is as old as evolving Spirit. This publication is not for those who doubt, it is for those who seek, for to doubt can only close the doors of consciousness, usually through fear. With the philosophy we have there is no need for fear, unless it is the wrath of God you fear and then that fear is only momentary as no sooner do you think this than the philosophy will clarify that God is only love and why should love be feared! My good friends it is with the utmost respect for your beliefs that I must tell you that to equate this that is being given with what has been given before would only be a waste of good energy, rather give some small time to thinking about what is contained within the covers of this humble book, given this time I think that you will find the effort, small as it is, worthwhile. Spirit attempts always to supply what is asked for. Maybe your specific request has not been met in this publication, maybe you haven't requested yet, however there is an answer for every one ask or not.

This time has been an interesting one for you were slow to hear our call and then you expect us to be prompt to yours, this is purely jest, we realise the difficulties that you experience. Go now with the peace of the Divine Lord, may He bestow you with many blessings.

WORDS FOR A WINTER SOLSTICE.

Friends it is the night of the Light, an evening for the re-dedication of one's self to fulfilling the wishes of God, the one and only true Light. When one sees that the flame is a representation of the true Light then one must realise that every time, they light their candle they in that act reaffirm that it is with the help of God that they may have their duty fulfilled.

To think that we tread this earth alone is not a wholesome thought, but to realise, we are but a small part of a very large whole then the feeling is of a very different nature. As you gather here this time it is with sincerity, a sincerity that is immediately recognised by God who immediately sends us to be close by you to be ever of help to you in the struggle back to Him. Light your candle, see the flame gather strength, feel the closeness of Spirit and realise that you have summoned the help of God Almighty and that help has arrived. It is suggested that you keep your special candle for those occasions where special help is needed. If you find that your candle burns out then with the last part lighting, light a fresh candle and dedicate this new candle as you have dedicated this candle this night. Light times are ahead for many wonderful events are to happen. There are plans afoot that can only be implemented when harmony exists. You have listened to all that we have had to impart up to now and this has been well.

The function of this information is to enable you to accept that there is a future with Spirit and that we do not desert you when you appear to be doing well. No, we stay with you in some form or other that best befits the concepts you are able to understand. This time we do not bring you warnings or tough questions no we bring you hope, hope of a nature that Spirit still wants you to carry on until all experiences for this lifetime have been met. It is not always possible to attain this degree of success during one's sojourn on earth but it is still possible to complete a reasonable cycle of experience whilst in that state.

The next stage in the evolution of the Spirit after the stage on earth is not quite as appealing as one would hope to expect. Do not read into this any fears of hell fire or the like, no what is been spoken of is that the need still exists the go further towards the Light that even though you have taken a step nearer to God then you are no great distance closer for there is no measure for that growth, it takes many experiences before an appreciable step can be taken. This may appear to give you no hope, but heed these words and realise that the next stage of growth from this point of view is immense, it is only in the realisation in the next world that one can perceive in a greater fashion the distance that one has yet to go. An example of this is if at this stage you were to be told that a great number of years must elapse before you were to realise a dream and that during this time you would undergo much turmoil, you would certainly hesitate before you set foot on that path, that is if you would ever. In the evolvement of the Spirit the measure is eternity, rest assured that this is the only place that you have time, then in timelessness eternity is not necessarily long. It is difficult to comprehend this but it is difficult for us to give this to you in an understandable fashion. It is important to understand this for then you will have the ability to change hopelessness into hope.

We will leave you with this little exercise for tonight, learn to understand that there is only hope, no hopelessness when measured on the scale of eternity. With this we take our leave and leave you in the care of the Light that you have dedicated yourself to this night, to the care of the Light, to the love of the Light, to the work of the Light, and may the Light in all wisdom give that to you that you so much need, the love of God, the only true Light. God blesses you all.

PRAYER.

My friends, it is strange that though so much has been said regarding the future of humankind that nothing has been said how much can be achieved through simple prayer, in fact the future of humankind depends of the simplest prayer, "Dear God that I may see your Light." With this prayer we make a deliberate dedication to the Father in so far that it is our life that we wish to be led in an illuminated fashion. We also by this prayer earnestly request that God by showing His Light will illuminate the path for us to follow.

God is the only source of such guidance though He will appoint those who will carry out this task in the best way. There would be no sense in sending one that would not be understood. This misunderstanding would be because of the elevation in the spiritual ranks of the giver in relation to the level of the receiver. This is why we come to you for we are trained communicators and carry God's word.

There is no question but you have asked for the illumination that we have to give, God hears all prayers. There has also been a reason why all the questions have been raised with you up to now, you can now understand your own motivation in a much clearer way and can therefore understand better the path that you wish to follow. There are still some who dally on the path and until these catch up on the path, we cannot progress any faster. We have begun to talk on the subject of prayer so now let us continue, mankind has very fixed ideas on how to pray. It is not sufficient to recite verbatim some ritualistic conglomeration of words and expect results that in no way reflect in the words uttered. Many of the regular prayers said, or recited, tell God of the beliefs of humankind, or how much humankind knows of God or again how great God is. In reality what use do you feel these words to be, particularly if you recognise God as being all knowing. Let's consider the purpose of your prayer. If it is a dedication of your life to God so that you may be guided back to Him or a dedication of yourself to the works of God, then why not understand what it is you wish to say, and say it instead of trying to dress your prayer in frills in an attempt to make it seem more "holy". No, nothing can be truer than the truth, say what you mean.

The reason we like to write in this way is that the truth can be maintained and therefore the full power of the word can be felt. You will notice how these words no matter how often they are read impart a deeper meaning and increased understanding, such is the power of the word. So remember when giving of yourself in prayer that the words you use must be meaningful and for a purpose, and in all sincerity, for then and only then can they be understood and accepted on this plane and presented to God on your behalf.

We will finish this teaching with a thought; if we were to say pray with words, we did not mean then how would we feel if that prayer were answered for us in a way we didn't want? Would we blame God for not understanding what we meant, would we blame God for being stupid and carrying out our wishes? Most probably, and all the time the fault would be in the incorrect use of words. Spirit understands the words you use. Spirit will respect your wishes. Spirit will know what you mean but as you requested something else Spirit will have to respect your request.

Attend to the word and pray clearly. Remember we are always in attendance and only too glad to be of assistance to you in fulfilling your needs. We leave you now in the hands of the Father most high, He who is the Master Creator, He who is God, may He offer you every blessing. This is our prayer.

NEEDS AND WANTS (2).

Friends it is with the wish to be of service to God that we approach you this time. It would be impossible to impart that which we have to give you were it not for the devotion to the task that has been generated by those who have found the strength to persist with an understanding of the subject under discussion, namely where and why are we going the way we are going.

When last we spoke it was about prayer and it has been noted that many have gained a better understanding of the way to pray. Let it be said that a greater understanding has been developed by you as we can now understand one and another better and can therefore function as a closer unit in our work. So this time we shall talk a little further on the matter of needs and the association needs have with wants.

It is more common to have wants than needs, the reason being that so often our needs are met automatically by those who care for us. Greed is the overriding factor that rapidly develops into craving and eventually emerges into the consciousness as a "need". This "need" appears so great that it imposes a certain dominance over us and by some extension can even dominate to the extent that murder could be committed to achieve the end of attaining the object of our craving. It is only necessary to look at the common habit of cigarette smoking, where the craving is so strong that nothing will be allowed to replace the cigarette, not food, not love, nor any urgent need. Everything becomes subservient to the cigarette. "But I need to smoke," is the common cry, we have all heard it said, if this is a need how is it that so many survive without it, and how many die because of it. The physical needs of humankind are few, the spiritual needs are fewer and more simple, yet, man in his way fails to see this and as a consequence occupies himself developing more fads to add to his "needs" list.

First of all, it would be a good exercise if one were to get a pen and paper and make a list of the needs of their body; the need of food; the need of cover; the need of sleep etc. See how long the list gets. Next go through the list and recheck to see if there are any wants there; do you really need all that has been listed? If on the recheck you find no wants listed then you need to check again, - didn't you. You now see how impossible it is to separate initially the needs from the wants. Check again. Each time you check you will find that many of the needs you thought you had were just wants. What you need is to survive in this life. You may ask why. If you don't survive long enough to fulfil our spiritual needs then you have not used that which has been given to you to get that which is necessary to get closer to God. Surely this is the prime need. Earlier we said that the spiritual needs were simplest to achieve.

The Master Creator is perfection and for anybody to think that perfection would create an environment that was unsuitable for our requirements would be in a situation of ignorance. The simplest logic would indicate that the conditions that have been made for us are perfect for that purpose they were designed for, to support humankind so that a human can support it's Spirit and get a closer understanding of the task in hand and thus fulfil it's obligations to this incarnation. The one great flaw in the way things are now is that humankind has the need to learn and therefore has the need to take responsibility for itself. To do this humankind needs to have free will for only then can it assimilate the understanding of this learning. Humankind introduces the flaws due to a reluctance to take this responsibility and goes off on a divergent path.

Too many times we see how humankind finds it necessary to hide its misdeeds through acts like abortion etc., another endless list. It is only by the recognition of the needs and to take responsibility for them that humankind can progress. Understand that there are many more words used in telling lies than in telling the truth. When we find a need to speak chose the truth. There is less waste of words, time and energy telling the truth than in trying to create a lie. Again, in the terms of needs and wants see that there is so much waste in pandering to wants, an animal's body lies rotting, wasted, just because somebody somewhere wanted its coat. Look there, a child's body awaits disposal unwanted just because somebody wanted sex. We know that these words are harsh and brutal yet this is the truth as you have created it, not God. Go back to your list again. See that God's creation was perfect for the needs of humankind but that it is humankind who wants more, remember that you are human. Take responsibility for that role you have.

We will go now but not before we again emphasise our unlimited, unconditional love for you all. It is our sincerest wish that all will receive these messages in the way that they have been given, with that unconditional love and that God may bless all your efforts in attempting to achieve your goal and give you a greater understanding of your needs and wants.

God blesses you all.

EGO AND HUMILITY.

My dearest friends it is with a loving Spirit that I approach you this time. You will notice the added familiarity between Spirit and humankind that exists this time for have we not drawn that much closer. It is through these words that a bond can be formed stronger than any other bond, a bond with God, through an understanding that has never existed before, at least in this lifetime on this earth.

We feel that now you can be more at one with us but we would stress that a constant referral to the words that have been given before be maintained. There were warnings there that must be heeded and understood. It so often happens that a certain complacency sets in and the signs are not noticed. Incursions of negativity can be made into your knowledge that leave it vulnerable. When the consequential crises occurs, you are unprepared and are then open to the abuse that negativity has in store for you.

Again, let us look at the ego. The ego is sneaky in that it approaches under the heading of being of service to others. In other words, in doing good you become a "do gooder". A "do gooder' is one who does good but knows it and thereby lays a condition that the act must be also recognised by others and favour given to the doer. Therefore, the work ceases when the recognition ceases. This is indeed the folly that persists with those who suffer from ego; they are only available if there is a cause that will make them appear great in the minds of others. Be aware that ego does not recognise any barriers only those that seek to confine its own egotistical development. Then it approaches the obstacle taking what it can for its own glory. When that is to be no more glory the egotist escapes before the real work is just about to begin, leaving the cause short-handed and in a state where failure is inevitable. All the good has already been removed and absorbed by the ego, and when the failure takes place the egotist crows that it couldn't survive without them. If the cause still survives in spite of the egotist then the cause is now wrong, that is to say in the words of the egotist, "something must be wrong as it was doomed when I left." And so it goes on and on.

We must constantly check where we are; there must be no let-up in the constant vigil for ego such is this insidious emotion. The medals that are to be won are all in this world, the Spirit world, not in yours. Your world is a place of work, that is why you chose it. You are there for experience not glory. Glory is for God; humility is for you.

Go now exercising the knowledge of this matter, look not to others to find this fault, look to yourself for it is there that it needs recognition and removing. If all were to observe this than all would be acting in a state of humility.

Next, we shall speak of humility, this is well worth exercising. Work on the fundamental principle that no human has power from God; there may be a case to recognise that where power exists with the human, it is only of an earth nature unless it is of an evil nature. The nature of power in the human on earth is solely in the exercising the function of its own existence; in other words that they may live as a human being and does not extend to supremacy over others. Where one sees the wilful interference with the fundamental rights of others then one is witnessing the power of evil. To exercise this evil power, it is necessary to accept the ruling of the dark ones, and we know where that leads us, back to where we came from. So why step backwards and waste the effort spent on getting this far, where ever that is. So now you see that the most important observation to make in this context is to recognise the potential of egotism, recognise the location and function of power, and thus you will find your own humility. When praised for work done remember "thanks be to God".

When tempted to seek power remember that this is why you are here, you tried this one before. Remember that the only power you have is in the exercising of free will. Finally remember that you and only you have the power to get yourself back to God. Exercise your free will and make that choice, and hopefully we will all meet there, next to God. With these words I leave you this time and pray that they will be of illumination for you on your path. May God in all His Majesty confer all blessings on you, to give you the strength that you need for your task.

POWER.

Friends this time we will talk some more about power and how to achieve it. Yes, it is power we talk of but perhaps not the power you think it is. There are many types of power, the power of speech, the power of the ruler, the power of electricity; yes, many types of power, the power of evil, the power of God, many types of power. The power we talk of is the power that is for humankind, the power to get back to God and all that encompasses.

There are many aspects to this power and perhaps if you understand it better you will appreciate what it is you should be doing and be satisfied with that. So often the human seeks to posses the power that is the power that is God's alone. Why should he confuse this with any other power? This is a particularly important question for the answer is simply that he shouldn't. The power that the human must concentrate on is that which is for him to use. This is a very uninteresting power in that it is only to be used on oneself and only over one's self. It cannot be used to the good over others, as that would be inflicting your will on them. It cannot be used for the good over others for they have their own power that is particular to themselves and for you to use your power over them is also judging them not to have any ability of their own, nor the ability to use it in their own way. You will see in this latter statement that the ability to use the power you have is strictly confined to yourself unless it is your wish to go outside those boundaries and impose what you see as being best for others. But who are you to judge especially as you appear not to even know what you have yourself never mind having the knowledge how to use it?

Next, we will see why and how that power works for oneself if properly exercised. In the first place we are given all that is necessary to enable us to return to God. We have been given the power to know right from wrong, the power to reason. It is with this power of reason that we can understand the true purpose of our time on the earth plane. When in Spirit existence that sense of reason still persists. We use it in many ways; we use it to decide to do certain things in order that we may become exposed to situations that will lend themselves to providing the necessary experience that we entered the earth plane to achieve. So now you see that the use of this power is, in a sense, to help us in our evolvement towards the Light and for no other reason. This power we speak of is peculiar to the human species and a different power is for the other species. It is the human that needs to evaluate.

Next use of this power is in making decisions. We need to understand our needs and decide how best to satisfy them. This takes some power and yet more to implement the motion that will allow the necessary happening to take place.

There is also a further use of power, the combined power of a number who gather in the Light for the work of the Light. Their power is combined with the power of those who guide them in the particular endeavour that they seek to serve, and this combined power can then be so strong, taking in the energies of at least two existences, that of the earth and that of Spirit. We would like to make it very clear at this stage that in the latter situation it is only by clear commitment on the part of the Spirit incarnate on the earth plane together with that of its physical body that Spirit can accept this unification of powers. Again, we would stress that caution be applied, for to enter into an arrangement such as this without clear knowledge of the undertaking would be pure folly. This is why Spirit continuously stresses the need for the human to retain his power for himself and when he has gained full knowledge of its implications uses this power to embark on a combined power path with Spirit.

Many have fallen victim to the power struggle the human has with those forces that are not of God. This again is an area where those working on a psychic plane need to be particularly wary insofar that they can easily be deluded into false senses of power. Witchcraft is such an area whereby power is promised to the participant in exchange for the power of the participant with the premise that it is to be used for the benefit of others. Unfortunately, the participants do not fully realise the full implications of their actions in that there are other conditions involved that have not been made clear. When the realisation that all is not well occurs it also becomes apparent to the hapless victim that they have no power to remove themselves from their predicament since they gave their power away in the first place, might we add by their own free will.

We feel that this is sufficient outline of power and all you should need to know for a while yet. So, if you like the basic rules could be: (1) don't seek power, you already have it given to you by God, (2) use your power solely to your own benefit, in getting you back to God, (3) when you understand, you can combine your power but be sure it is with the Light that you do it, and (4) remember that it is your ultimate decision how you use that power that you have been Divinely given. Use it with wisdom. This wisdom we seek to share with you is for the purpose of helping you in those moments of crisis that occur from time to time. We are your friends in Spirit and seek only to be of your assistance in the name of God Almighty, The True Light, and in His name, we invoke all blessings for you.

Go in peace and love.

RESOLUTIONS.

My friends it is very hard to add to what has already been given before regarding this season. It is above all else a time for rejoicing for it is the eve of the year to come. We have spoken regarding time but in this instance, it is those on earth that make significant gestures of time that we in Spirit cannot ignore. Yes, this is the fresh beginning when many resolve to avoid the pitfalls that they fell afoul of previously.

A noble attempt to change is always appreciated. In this instance of new resolve, it is mostly words that are used so as to conform to popular trends and not to form a firm resolve. Let us look at the true significance of this season of Christmas and new year. We have viewed this time from one perspective now let us gather the lessons that can be learned throughout this period. The first advice is for observations to be made of the behaviour of those about you. Judge others not, rather take the image they portray and look as into a mirror with their portrait superimposed on your image. See that you lack the necessary lustre that would indicate that you are not tarnished similarly to the superimposition, for are you not all human? Take this as the truth and see yourself no greater than any man. Rather see yourself as every other man, vulnerable to the temptations of that which can be termed negative. We would suggest that it might be a time for taking cognisance of the progress or lack of progress that we, you and us, have caused during the last yearly period. This you can accomplish by measuring yourself against all that you observe during the Christmas season. If you have judged yourself in earnest you will then realise the matters that most need attention during the coming year. Observe these and with firm resolve effect the changes that you will find necessary.

On the road to God the key to evolvement is awareness. This awareness can help us to work closer together. Notice firstly that as we in Spirit have to honour your free will it is therefore only by the subtlest of signs that we can attract your attention. By your awareness we have a much easier task. Take an example of the man who feels the insignificance of a sneeze as heralding the onset of a cold, this enables him to seek attention for his malady and thereby reduce the consequences of ignoring the sneeze and the possibility of developing pneumonia. A simple demonstration of how you may enter this period of celebration with the new knowing that has been imparted to you. Remember that we are in constant attendance on you and should you feel the need to call us we will be here for you. No reason is too trivial for if it causes you pain than we would wish to be at your assistance. We leave you in God's Grace and Light and call on Him to bestow upon you all His Heavenly Blessings.

REFLECTIONS.

It is as your year comes to its end that thoughts turn in unison seeking enlightenment for what is to come. It is also a time to reflect on the same time of the last year when you underwent a similar exercise. Take notice of your previous reflections and notice that there are some of the same thoughts appearing in the current reflections. Now what does this indicate? Does this indicate that there is a lacking on our behalf in Spirit or does it rather reflect a reticence on your part to avoid the responsibility that is solely yours? Do we hear you say that Spirit had made promises then that were never fulfilled? Do we hear you say that Spirit has not given you any assistance in finding your path in life? Do we hear you say that you have been misled by Spirit? Do any or all of these hypothetical questions appear in any way familiar to you? If they do they are no longer hypothetical are they? No, they are real and must not be ignored.

If you choose to treat Spirit in this way then that is your folly for Spirit has no need to do any of the things that you would be accusing it of. What advantage is it to Spirit to mislead or misguide you in any way? To take offence to the questions would also be a silly way, for the accusations have no relevance to Spirit

But humankind cannot afford to ignore them for in their utterance humankind has laid open all human short comings. It is those who talk against Spirit that show themselves as lacking knowledge and they will appear as the fools.

We implore you to observe the shortcomings in your past year and acknowledge that the only reason it might have lacked fulfilment would be due to your own faults manifesting in whatever way they it did. It is with this idea that we leave the subject of the year past, leave it there in the past and only take with you the lessons of that period that bear a relevance to this that is to come. Be aware that in a spiritual sense that there is little that one can take from that period but yet that is the essential part. Remember too that had that year been your last on this earth there would also have been little for you to bring into your eternity.

This year coming, though it will not be your last, and we wish to reassure you of this point, should be treated as though it were going to be. Notice how you will change your priorities so as to compensate for all those years that no cognisance of the spiritual side of your nature was taken. Now the picture changes, how many need to be taken to the very edge of the grave before they realise the purpose of life on earth? How many then take note and renew their understanding? Sadly, very few, even as they look into their grave, they blame others of being blind and never understand that it is themselves who lack the sight. Friends it causes sadness that so many behave thus and the work of Spirit is to little avail.

This time it is our intention that more will avail of the help from Spirit and more will thank God for their salvation. Go forth as emissaries of the Lord God for you have been privileged to be enlightened. Do not forget that it was your choice that all has taken place. You have chosen to heed the Word; you have made the Word flesh.

Go now in the grace of God reflecting on all that has been said in His name. May God rest you all and give you peace and Light.

BADNESS.

Yes, we have called, for you gave us the request for more words and there are many to give. We see that the words given recently were of much benefit to those who read them. It is in terms of imparting knowledge that the full purpose can be understood. There is no room for idle chatter, as time is not there for the wasting nor is the energy that is to be used. It is better that we remain constantly aware of the questions you need to be addressed.

Many have found that the lessons of life have been of great illumination yet many then switch off the Light and return to their old unlit ways resting on the knowledge that they have been allowed to experience. Now experience is not for collecting and then to be stored unused, no, knowledge is to be gained, experienced, and then applied to your existence so then more knowledge can be gained. In this way knowledge can be understood as a living experience not only as an experience in living. You can now see that all that is good or bad can be deemed as knowledge for it is all valuable but the important point that must be recognised is that all knowledge has a use in your everyday living, good or bad. How, you may ask, can bad have a place? Firstly, we must understand the term bad. Definition tells us that any experience that is of a negative nature is considered bad. You will remember we spoke on the subject of sin where we stated that there are no levels of sin rather a different degree of consequence? So too with badness, it has only a different degree of consequence. You may measure badness in the way it effects not only you but also others. Badness in experience if considered correctly can show us without any doubt how good things could be. Again, let us look at the hypothetical case of learning how hot a hot poker is. Let us first take the hot end. The important point is the degree to which it burns and the positive result of this silly act is the level of understanding we have attained. We now know that hot pokers burn, even cripple, but we also learn to never bother to handle a hot poker again. By other experiments with a hot poker, we can even find that it has many other uses that are in no way negative and that it was only as to the use the poker was put to that deemed the act bad. There are many experiences in life that in their essence are not bad but the way their usefulness is exploited by humankind decides the category the use would fall into, good or bad.

Let us look now to misuse. Misuse is wrong as it turns good into bad. It can also turn bad into good but this action perhaps is not called misuse by the powers of positivity. Misuse of the abilities of Spirit are the gravest sin that any being can commit. We take specific cognisance of the events that have already been manifested in the area of Spiritual Healing. To heal so that the ego of the administrator may be fed is wrong on all counts and we can only advise that this grievous act does one thing and one thing only, it allows the "healers" to destroy themselves. Healing may take place but this is only due to the mercy of God who understands that the recipient of the healing deserves to be healed but has been used by the "healer". Misuse of this ability only allows the egotist to become even more egotistical until finally they succumb to this self-administered poison. You will remember we have talked before on this matter.

There are many other ways that egotists seek to feed their habit, a habit which can be more difficult to overcome than other addictions. It is unfortunate that it is in the area of spirituality that this event occurs as it has also the effect of driving the receiver of such "benefit" to trust less when they realise that they have been fooled by the ego feeder, and in the name of God. It is not sufficient to light a candle and openly profess that all is done in the name of God, realise that to the egotist they are god. So therefore, all that has been done is in the name of ego. If you wish to work in the true Light then you must be conscious of this ego and be even more conscious of the God you wish to honour. You have to be aware of humility and that all is to be in the name of the one true Light. If you feel that you are reasonably aware that there is a channel that has this clarity then you may consider making the request for illumination on the subject you feel drawn to. If you are the recipient of the knowledge that enables you to be a channel then you may indeed practice.

You will be aware from time to time that you will be tested so that you may realise when you are not, or that you are, functioning on the correct basis. If you find that there is any way you do not attain the standard necessary then you must immediately cease the performance in the name of God. If you do not cease then you will find that the ability will be removed from you as the Supreme will not permit His name to be used in connection with any action that could be detrimental to another being seeking to evolve back to the Light. So, we are again back to the definition of the act. Now you understand that though the ritual has been performed that it is indeed God who administers the grace, but the performer of the ritual has to take responsibility for the effects the ritual may have on them. Therefore, if the performer does not seek through the proper channels or for the proper reasons then he must accept the consequences.

There is also another level that may be operated on and that is unfortunately where many egotists arrive at. This level is operated by those who have not evolved sufficiently to work within the Light and seek constantly to keep the consciousness of others on the same level as themselves or to reduce others so that they are no better than these lowly creatures. These latter can perform many of the phenomena that many in the Light perform. The results are not the same.

To finally end this writing for this time we would like to remind all who seek to work within the Light to be aware of all the traps that are set for the unwary. We seek to enlist the aid of many to work for the only God there is for all. We seek no more then you would answer our call and that we all may attain the harmony that is necessary for the work that is on hand. We thank you for the facility that you have extended to us. Yes, we are those who work with your healing and have been permitted to communicate with you in this manner in this instance. Keep the Love of God foremost in your mind and forever dwell in His Light.

THE SPIRIT LIFE.

My friends it is with a certain hope that we come, and it is with certain hope that we find our way into your midst. Many have found that their orthodox teaching has been challenged but this is not the case. When one finds that their belief has been shaken then it is a normal reaction for them to feel in some way insecure, do you? There is no need to have any fear for if you challenge the words that have been given then in honesty you will find that the tenets of your thinking have not really been affected.

When we come to you it is through the word of God and through the love of God. The basis of our teaching has been always the same for it is directed for the same purpose, your return to God. My friends do not fear the shake you feel for it will only shake the cobwebs from your mind and help you realise that all can now begin to be understood. We find many minds closed to us, for the power of the material life has caused the minds of humankind to close. It is our intention to shake off the shackles of materialism and to dress yourselves in the cloth that is more natural to you, to fashion a new cloak, a cloak of spirituality.

When you realise all this, then perhaps you will feel more confident with the words we have to give.

Now we will talk further on the questions that have been raised regarding this life you now lead and the life you face in your future. Now we are aware of the life around us and how we sense the difficulties that confront us. Our difficulties are not of the nature you would recognise, but none the less present themselves as difficulties in this place. Now when first confronted with troublesome situations we too feel that same feeling that you face when confronted with a new experience. We too quake with our fear. We too worry with our worry. We too seek guidance. So is there is a difference. Yes, it is the level of difficulty that is different, and the fear, and the worry. The guidance is the same in that it can help us to overcome our fear and cease the worry.

You wonder where then is the reason for wishing to enter this world if it is no better than the one you are in. There is a very good reason to wish for this evolvement, and that is that you are closer to God. Take for example the world you live in. In the material sense you seek to work for somebody and whilst in that employment you seek to climb the ladder, so that eventually you will be closer to the god you have given your allegiance to. The difference you will experience is therefore; that the place you have earned is only temporary, in other words only for the length of your useful life. There are difficulties also, the ones at the bottom of the ladder have their troubles, the ones higher up have also difficulties but different and so on up the ladder. Again, we will remind you that the difference is that your rise up the ladder comes to an end earlier than the end of your life, leaving you time to reflect on the areas that you had for so long neglected. You have the time to realise that you had left so much until then, and question the availability of time in which to take notice of that which is necessary to fulfil your spiritual requirements from the life you have left to live. In many instances there is no time left. In our case when we evolve to this level, we find that so much from the earth life is applicable, and that, had we had the understanding available to us, we would have found that there was more we could have done with our earth incarnation that would have strengthened us so much more.

The difficulties we encounter are not really more difficult than the difficulties you experience but it is a question of relevancies. The important point we wish to make is that all experiences we seek in the world of the material are to help us understand better the position we now occupy. The effort that is needed to assimilate the knowledge is no less than that which is needed in your existence. You probably feel that this again makes evolvement pointless, when you think that we are no better off than you. Think again. Firstly, we are closer to God, secondly, we have a greater understanding of the task that confronts us, thirdly we realise that we could be in a better position had we paid greater attention to the facilities that earth incarnations presented us with. Like you we floundered around in the mess there, patting one another on the back, we were all in it together. Like you we sought the easy way through life and like you we saw the folly in our ways, when eventually we had to face the consequences of our stupidity. Yes, we remember only to well and we re-live those memories through you.

We seek to guide you through your life to help you experience that which you came to experience and in turn we experience your experiences also. We feel your sorrow, we feel your happiness, we feel your depression, and we feel your joy. We know what life is all about, but we would not want to find it necessary to experience in the flesh again. Would you in your world like to find yourself once again at the bottom of the ladder? We don't want to have that experience either. We would like if you would listen more to the guidance you are given, that you become more aware of the path you are on, become more aware of the experiences you seek, have more courage, have greater trust in those who you seek to guide you, and above all have a greater feeling for the love that God sends you. If you heed these words you can certainly achieve a greater evolution than if you were to choose to ignore them. You would not then have to face such great difficulties in your future and on arriving here you would have a much clearer view of God. Take us into your everyday life, allow us to be your guide, take us into your home, your work, for then you carry the eternal flame of God to all men.

Go with Gods love.

SIN (1).

It is on a serious note that we come this time for there are matters arising within this Centre that need to be attended to. As before Spirit was aware of the goings on in the minds of people. It is not a matter of prying, for the guardian of those who would seek the aid in the matter in hand, would seek the help of others involved in guardianship to sort out the irregularities that were occurring.

Now we are informed that there are indeed irregularities occurring and would like to ask those who are becoming involved to seek only that which is for them, and to let those who would seek to undermine their confidence look to themselves. We also would like to let the perpetrators know that they are the fools, for it is known what they seek to do. Now some may accuse these writings of being unspiritual, they come from Spirit, Spirit from the Light so how can they be unspiritual? Heed these words for they are not for wasting.

Now we shall speak of matters more pertinent to the individual who seeks enlightenment, though that is not to say that the previous words were not enlightening. This Centre is instituted by Spirit, run by Spirit for those Spirits who seek the way out of the maze of darkness that humankind has permitted to be grown. There is no way that Spirit can be distracted from this task. It is only when there are no more prepared to take the path that Spirit will stop this work. You will notice that we said `prepared' for if the ideal for humankind in the humans mind is ignorance then that is what humankind wishes and humankind must therefore be prepared to face the consequential action of these ways they have chosen. There is only one way, though many paths, back to God and that is by determination. If one seeks to return to God but only with certain provisions then that will be the way he will return, only in a certain way and provisionally, it doesn't take much wind to dislodge a loose slate.

Let us now examine the matter of sin. You are taught there are many kinds of sin, this is not so. Sin is sin and there is no excuse for it other than there is a different degree of consequence for the sinful action. Every cause has an effect. Let us look at the push used to move an object, a little push moves the object only a little and a hard push moves it further. If you look at this analogy closer you will also understand that the mass of the object will cause the movement of the object to differ as the mass differs. So, to with sin, the degree of seriousness (push) is proportional to the degree of consequence (mass of object), but the sin has still been committed. Therefore, we can now see that there is no way that sin can be evaluated into `kinds'. The simple answer is to avoid sin as much as is humanly possible and then there is no need to try and justify the mal-action. This brings us to understand how we cope with the knowing that we have transgressed. This is infinitely more complicated as this is the effect that conscience has on the offender. Working on the understanding that the offender is even conscious that he has misbehaved, then in his own judgement on himself he will punish himself by the pangs of conscience that he suffers, provided that he has the honesty to face himself. Should he be one of those who seeks always to lay the blame on others then there is no punishment on this earth of yours that would suffice the need to right the wrong, for that need is not recognised. This latter is unfortunately too common.

We see then that sin is always wrong and that the matter of making amends has often to be held until the sinner reaches the level of consciousness that exists in the world or worlds that come to you when you leave the one you are on. There are ways to make amends but these we shall speak of when the recognition of the wrongs is adopted and better understood. We feel that you have sufficient to ponder on for this moment. Go now in the peace and love that God has provided for you, without condition, sinner or no. God blesses you all.

SIN (2).

It is strange that all the will in the world is insufficient to quell the personification of evil that is requested to be kept maintained by humankind. We in the purity of God's Light see many intrusions into the beauty that has been created for you through the blessings of God. It is a fact that humankind seeks continuously to brand its image over the image of God and to indeed see themselves as the creators of the universe, where as they (humankind) have only created the tangible world that the human seeks to exist within.

Notice must also be taken of the inbuilt controls of the situation that humankind has also created. Were they not able to control then they would not feel the satisfaction of the niche of power that is for them alone to have but also to wield over others. One has only to look to the large overpowering institutions that have been created to service the greed of humankind and the power that has been fostered by them over those who have helped in their creation. Is it not strange that even in this situation that there is no sense of loyalty amongst the wielders of power, only continuous struggle to have power over one another? They do not even realise that the power they are subservient to is as invisible as the power itself, though exists none the less. It is important that an understanding is achieved of this situation.

One way to realise the full implication of this power is to draw comparisons between the power of God and this power of humankind. See that God seeks to continuously manifest Himself whereas the human seeks to conceal his power until the "right time" and then to use it as an expression of his own strength and in order to gain further power over his fellow human. Whereas again God only seeks to show humankind the power that is available for them to see God and to identify the path they must take in order to safely return to him.

This return to God is a story of love tolerance, mercy, guidance, peace, harmony. No other story can ever encompass so many aspects for the unfoldment takes a lifetime. There is no need at any time to know and understand the complete story but to realise that one is indeed one of the principal characters in the story and to pray they are the hero.

EARTH LIFE.

It is the time now to discuss the nature of one's time spent in the unreal world of the earth incarnation. Many, when they first encounter the earth existence, get totally engrossed in the finery that presents itself to their senses and consequently fail to recognise the true purpose of their existence on that plane. On their return to the reality that is known as Spirit life they then realise the folly of the existence that they have just left. On the basis of the clarity of knowing the true nature of their purpose they resolve once again to attempt to complete their evolution in a speedy fashion.

It is a difficult task that they face and though they earnestly seek to conform to the rules they adopt to help them, they find that your world is so unreal for them that they lose sight of their direction, rather like a child in a fairyland. When the reality of the Spirit world is presented to them, they see it as unreal because the tangible world to them is the one that their physical senses respond to. It is necessary that they at some stage discover the way things are; that the body is only a transient vehicle for the Spirit to exist in for a short space in time; that the immortality is for the Spirit and that the body is in fact their mortal self. One does not see a suit of clothes as always existing; you realise that it has a certain life span dictated by the quality of the cloth, how you treat it and how the fashions change. You do not allow the suit of clothes dictate to you how you must behave, what direction you must take, how long you should live; no, it is just a suit of clothes. To your Spirit your body is just a suit of clothes and like a suit you chose it for a particular purpose. You know that you would not wear a working suit into an environment that was not suited to it. As with clothes in a physical sense, so it is with your body in a spiritual sense. You are aware in the physical way that the suit must be cared for so that it will be able to serve its function, you maintain it, and so too with your body you must also maintain it. The Spirit must not let the body rule it and dictate what is best for it; the body is of the physical world and does not have any knowledge of the spiritual world. To the body the world it is in is the real world, it is the Spirit that realises differently. As a spiritual being you too must realise your real world is the Spirit world and that the body is in a way your passport to the various experiences that you need for the advancement of your understanding of your reality.

You are aware of the times while you are in the earth environment that you feel a need to step back from the task you are performing so that you may have a clearer perspective of the work you are engaged in. This exercise is also very valuable to your Spirit, meditation gives you this opportunity. When you meditate and get into that relaxed state allow your Spirit the facility to step from the body in order to survey the work in hand, and from a new perspective be better able to see its progress along life's path. Realising that the Spirit has this facility, and if one makes this conscious effort, then one must also accept that which they see as being the truth, for one, if genuinely seeking the truth, must surely do so in a true manner, a spiritual manner, for has it not been said that the truth is in Spirit. The next meditation that you engage in after reading these words be aware of the reason that you sit. In general meditation the purpose is for self-enlightenment, be enlightened. Leave the time for work to its time. Sit not for development, sit to evolve, sit to evolve spiritually. There is no time for experimenting so as to have that which no other has. What purpose would that achieve on a long-term basis, a long term like eternity? Having succeeded in achieving that which you sought it would be only a matter of one other reaching the same goal, then its uniqueness has been lost. That would be no achievement, if after such a short space of time your joy was lost.

No, seek not in that fashion, for the joy of spiritual achievement is in the sharing with others the pleasure of all having attained the same goals. There is no competition for there is space for all and time for all. One must realise the enormity of Spirit for it can encompass all and still have room left for itself, think of how large that must be for surely this is a description of God, a description of our purpose, a description of the very essence of ourselves, to be part of that described.

There is no need to sit in meditation seeking to develop one or many of the abilities of Spirit for that is a natural process and requires no understanding as to how this should happen. All that is required is the fundamental understanding of Spirit. That will enable you to make the necessary commitment to the work of the Spirit and all that is needed will be provided and come from the right source, God.

So finally remember that others are not there with you in the flesh to be your guides other than to help you be aware that guidance is available, what you decide after that is your responsibility. Take that responsibility and be glad for is that not accepting the fundamental gift that God has given you. Do not give it away to others. Listen to the guidance that is given from the truth. Stay forever in God's light, seek not the glorification of any human seek only the glorious return to reality. Go now understanding that which you seek is in this reality and what can be more real than eternity. Go with God's love and blessing.

HUMAN NATURE AND THE SPIRIT WORLD.

It is with some reluctance that I come to you this time for even as I write there are those who do not heed the words that have already been spoken. However, there are also those who have harkened well to the teaching and not allowed themselves to fall to the ways of others and turned these words into idle chatter.

We will speak this time of this side of the nature of humankind. Again, we will look at the words already spoken; the value of the word is only in its reception by the listener. It is a shame that the efforts that are made to help these words, go unappreciated and that they are not quoted often enough nor discussed often enough. These words are not just for one, to be filed away and never attended to again. These words are the living testimony to the existence of Spirit, to the Spirit that lives in every reader, to the Spirit that attempts to guide every reader. These words are the living testimony to the existence of God. Can you not accept them as such? If you can why then do you hide them away? Be aware that we are indeed with you and that we are aware of your call for help, as we are aware of your ignoring our response to your call. We might not always respond in the manner you want but we do respond.

There is another side to these words. There are those who treat these words with respect and it is an unfortunate fact that it is they who will take these words to heart. It is not the way it should be. We are not your judge; it is you who must judge you. To those who listen do not judge yourself too harshly, to those who do not listen, if you have troubled to read this far, be honest to yourself. Look at and judge yourself in the light of truth. Look not to others to judge them. You must learn first to look at yourself before you attempt to look at others, you will find that self judgement will keep you so occupied that there will be no time for the judgement of others. Now we have said enough on this matter. You have our love what else do you need? Oh yes, you find there is more you need. Well then listen. There is much to learn. To learn about the next level of Spirit would take many lifetimes of earthly incarnations and even then, full knowledge would not have been attained, for it is only by experience that full knowledge can be achieved. This is the reason that evolution is structured as it is. Many try to achieve full knowledge in one incarnation on earth yet that is really impossible. It is not even possible to achieve any great degree of evolvement by one incarnation in the next level of existence even though sufficient earth incarnations have been experienced. Now you can see why eternity is necessary. You can also hopefully see why you have to make such good use of the incarnation you are presently experiencing. You must always strive to attain that level of perfection that will hopefully take you that permanent step into the next level of experience.

The philosophy that now unfolds will take you the eternity to understand. We would like, at this stage, to help you to understand the basics of Spirit evolution. Firstly, understand that whatever concept you may have of God in the life you have at present is very inadequate but at the same time is sufficient for the present purpose. Let us draw your attention to feelings you have about things. You feel there is more to some understandings that you have. This is a true feeling for it is the latent knowledge that is of your Spirit that you are experiencing but this is not capable of being understood by your physical consciousness.

When you are finished with this present incarnation you will find yourself stepping into this world through that popular door, feared by the flesh, and known to earth consciousness as death. There has to be some way of making the transition from one level of existence to another. As the next world is not of an earthly physical nature your earth body would be useless. It is also to help the necessary awareness of the task in hand that the physical body is permitted to last the span of your earth life. In general, you will become aware of the impending transition from that life by the disintegration of the flesh-body. This next world you then face is but one step from the world you presently inhabit, that is why temporary visits can often be made to it by the temporary disembodiment of the Spirit. For example, this can happen during your sleep or during your meditation. In general terms it would be impractical to describe the world of Spirit to you, as so much would have to be left unsaid but we will try our best to work within acceptable terms.

We cannot tell you how beautiful life is here. It is so hard to even describe your next stage to you. Where we are is only barely understandable to you and we too find our future stages barely understandable. If we were to tell you that this is a land of love would you understand? The next stage of your evolution takes you into an existence that can only be described as such, a land of love. As you get closer to God so too do you get closer to His love. Your very being feels this love infusing into it. The degree to which you can absorb this love depends on the space you have left in your being for it to be felt by. If through your earth incarnation you have filled your self with the type of experience that is ungodly then you have limited the space that is available to God. When in your next state of existence, you find that you have caused the available absorption space to be limited then you will realise the folly in your previous existence, your earth incarnation, and require the opportunity to try and remove some of the dross from your being. Now this dross is related to your earth existence but you have desired to take it with you into Spirit where it has no value in any terms. It is necessary that you once again enter the earth world in order to shed it. Let us look at an analogy to explain the meaning of what we say. In your earth life there are many negative experiences that you take from childhood into adulthood. These experiences can affect your living in the more mature world that you then occupy. You find that it is necessary that you shed these negative experiences for you feel that they hold back your development as a maturing human being. You will then go about the necessary exercise or re-education of the self that will release the negativity that binds you. So too it is here, that in the light of the effect this negativity that hampers your spiritual absorption of the love of God and you will need for it to be removed from your being. You will require the facility to return to that stage of your being where you can relearn the required lessons and thereby release the negativity from your system.

It is felt that this is enough information for you at this time. You have certainly much to think about. We would suggest that you might focus yourself a little more on the love of God and we feel that this will help you be aware of a more positive approach to the existence you have at this present moment in your time. We go now but know that we have not left you empty handed. You may be sure that we will continue on this subject on another day. Go with the certain knowledge that you have the Love of God.

A PRAYER.

When you meditate you might include this little prayer? The words explain the circumstances.

"Dear God in your mercy, have pity on those poor souls who have digressed from the true path, to wander endlessly through the dark labyrinths, lost to the Light. Please God grant them another chance to see Your Illumination, so they may find their way back to You, realising their wrong, and forever live with You in perfect peace, harmony and love".

SPIRIT MIGRATION.

My friends, when last we spoke it was on the subject of the afterlife. You will notice that the expression "after life" is one that can only be used in the location you are presently at. A more apt expression for your situation would be the "in between life". You will understand that it is our wish to help you understand the situation in a true manner, so therefore it is essential that firm reference points are established. There is nothing firm about misnomers. From here on we must understand that the existence on the earth plane is but a transient stage in the migration of the Spirit back to its source, and that to have any other concept of this situation would not permit you to understand the reality. So now we can explore more clearly the full spectrum of Spirit migration.

Accepting that this present you are now in is but a stage in your journey, it is obvious that you will have a curiosity about what is to happen next. It is not the intention that we should give you a clear prospect of your future for then you would possibly avoid the difficult parts and thereby loose the potential to gain the necessary experience. You may discount the notion that life gets progressively harder or easier, the only progression is directly related to experience gained. Therefore, if you do not gain the correct experience through being aware of it the first time around then the experience will have to be more profound the second time in order that you may become more aware and subsequently will have to be even successively more profound, until the necessary experienced is gained. That would illustrate how then experience does not necessarily have to be harsh, rather awareness has to be acute.

So it is with earth incarnations, that they may be pleasant or harsh depending on your awareness. Awareness can be defined as the degree to which harmony exists between the body and the Spirit, the material and the spiritual. Be aware now of that which we have spoken about and sharpen your awareness by increasing your spirituality.

Now we may talk on other matters. This life you now live, incarcerated in the flesh, is but a short trial that you have necessary to bear until the time that you have achieved the experience you seek, through the tasks that you have set yourself. The trials you face are nothing to the suffering you experienced as a Spirit lost to the light. Yes, you were one of those that fell into that abyss. In the beginning there was perfect harmony but then like a disease the devil ego ran through the ranks of the Most High tearing it asunder. You have sometimes experienced this in your existence on earth; you have experienced it in this Centre. You were not cast from the heavens but you separated from the Light and took to your own path eventually finding your way into the dark labyrinth, lost. God in His Love permitted the Light to ever shine as a beacon to those who, one day, might raise their consciousness to acknowledge it and thereby find the way to return once again to the God they had so maligned. On seeing the Light you called out for the mercy that was for you, and found it. In this burst of

Illumination, you sought to return to God but not without your imposing conditions on the quality of being you should be, before you would feel adequate to again become part of that harmony. You examined yourself for many, many aeons before you could devise the plan that would be satisfactory to you and then and only then did you set out on the path you are still presently following.

We have spoken before of eternity and how it is inconceivable, it is enough to say that at this stage you would not wish to know where on that eternal path you are. Do not despair as yet you have travelled an immeasurable distance so far, so do not waste time by giving up. Should you decide that you cannot take anymore then be aware that you cannot go back for you would find you would only have to start again. Such is the attraction of the destiny you seek. It is only that at this stage you lack the awareness of the full extent of the task, you, by your own choice have undertaken. If you can accept that this is indeed the case then you must surely also be aware that there are definite ways that you must undertake to ensure that you will find the most efficient route. Now be aware that the way of knowing is through the understanding of spirituality, your spirituality, that you can understand the true meaning of this journey, a journey that is to take you through the ways of understanding the full extent of ego poisoning, a journey that has led you to this point in your time in your eternity. You will notice that no reference is made to others for each are in their own time and each have to understand their relationship to their own downfall, and each have to concern themselves with their own path, and each has to take responsibility for their own actions. It is for this reason that the message must be universal and can then contain certain references that do not necessarily refer to you, yet you must examine these before you discount them, for would it not be egotistical for you to feel they might not be applicable.

We will leave you for now so that you may have the opportunity to assimilate this knowledge that has been imparted to you in an attempt to share with you some of that which we have gained during our journey. We are not there yet and do not know how much longer it will take but we are aware that the path to God is well worth taking. It is in this knowing that we ask that God will continue to shine His Light in your direction ever Illuminating your path, ever encouraging you to return to the fold where His Love reigns for ever and ever. May God bless you.

WORDS TO A PSYCHIC.

You have posed many questions mainly directed towards my integrity. You must recognise by now that I am only the total of many and this you seek is therefore almost an impossibility as the questions are directed towards only one. We will however try and satisfy you in the clearest possible way.

Firstly, we would stress to you our honesty by stating that we seek only to bring to people of the earth a knowledge that will promote the truth behind the concept of a God migration, in other words a process that will help them in their return to the Light. It is not a true proposition that will dupe them into fooling themselves that they are any greater than they are. One must also be aware that there is no great formula that will answer all humankind. No one truth is the answer to all questions.

The dawning of the ages was marked by the downfall of Spirit beings. They fell into the darkness and it is from this quarter that we seek to help them rise. The question that was posed regarding direction, caution, protection, is really containing many parts that can be simply answered by realising that in order to return to God one has to emerge from the darkness into the Light. Now in the earth existence if one were to only recognise those who are in the Light then one would be ignoring all those who seek the help so that they too might emerge. Therefore, it is necessary that work should start in the dark, reaching for those who cry out, helping lift them into the shadows so that they can begin to adjust to the Light. To emerge at too fast a pace would only serve to dazzle. We hope that this explanation will suffice.

There are many that choose to ignore the fact of their early encounters with darkness and therefore ignore the lessons that were gained. The result of such a folly is a decreased sense of awareness of the operation of Spirit in coming from and going to the Light. Understand that it is the sole purpose of the earth existence that all fears and attractions for darkness are eradicated through knowledge. You also challenge the origins of our being, we are from the Light, does this suffice? Many would say yes but we know that you seek greater conviction. May we say this is noble but what would be more noble would be for the questions to be better understood by you. The question is an old one most often raised to challenge the beliefs of the questioner. One who asks this question has to understand that there is no finite answer as the comprehension of an earth incarnation is insufficient to understand the answer. However, we will give you a more elaborate answer. Humankind is formed for those Spirits who seek their return to God. We were once in that capacity. During successive incarnations we managed to find our path which eventually brought us to here. We are not evolved to even comprehend the finite outcome of our journey but let us say from our perspective we are in a better position to understand that we have a closeness to God, closer than ever before, at least within our own awareness.

We find that we have a memory that is becoming more familiar. Therefore, as we are closer to the Light, than you are on earth, we can therefore say we come from the Light. The other question tests our perception of God. Again because of our closeness to God we have the facility to have a greater understanding of the true meaning of God. We do not seek to impress you with our superiority nor allow you the position to feel that you have an intelligence that would allow you to nod your head in agreement. We will therefore agree with you that indeed God is the epitome of Love, Light, Goodness, Sacredness, Justice, Mercy, God the very essence of all our beings, without God nobody would be.

It is felt that these questions are directed more to help you understand yourself than to test us. The purpose of your sensitivity is only that you may use it in the assistance in helping others who lack understanding. Do you realise the folly in ignoring the true purpose of your incarnation? Let us help you further, we seek only in the development of your understanding of your purpose. We see that you have a misunderstanding of Spirit, Spirit origins, and your origins. Where do we start? Firstly, we must ask that you bear with us as we untangle the web that you have permitted to be wound around you. The disturbances you are feeling are the tugs that have tried to take you backwards. Realise that indeed Spirit-wise our worlds are not that different yet to you in the flesh it is indeed a great difference. When you left this world, you left much powerful knowledge behind you. This was a safety measure in case you found that you were not to be in a position to use it safely. This was the case until now.

Up to this time you have been out on a spiritual limb. You have functioned psychically and functioned well. However now is the time to study your true purpose. It is not your destiny to be a freak performing to amaze the public. Yours is a crusade in the enlightenment of many through the abilities of your spiritual powers. You think you know where you come from but you do not realise the enormity of the world of Spirit or of the many levels of thought that exists. We do not try to scold or correct you in any punishing way, indeed we cannot for we cannot sit in judgement, of any kind, on you. We would like to be as a friend to you and you to be our friend. Much work has to be done and as you are aware the changes that have taken place around you are just a preparation for this work.

The reason for us approaching you with such caution is so that we do not disturb you too much. You say you have no fear and we agree with that statement but we would advise you that it is within the power of the dark ones to instil fear in the unwary. This is why we constantly advise on there being an awareness of the dark side of nature, thus one may be aware of the closeness of the risk of losing one's direction. Many have regressed in this fashion, yes even some as evolved as you. We could spend much time discussing this subject but let us finalise this dissertation by again reassuring you that indeed we are from the one true Light of God; that we have the welfare of incarnated Spirit to the fore and that the world we inhabit is the world of Spirit; that we cannot operate outside the laws of God nor can we force our will on any human. In the end you must decide for yourself where your allegiance lies and until you do that you cannot expect to understand your purpose. Accept our love and the love of those who work with you. We hope that you find these words as they are given, in love, and for your illumination.

God blesses you.

MORE ON SPIRIT EVOLVEMENT.

My dear friends, many have read these words and yet many more have yet to awaken to their availability. Those who have received them and read them and absorbed into themselves the realisations must surely be aware of their benefit. Yet there are those of you that still hold these words outside of yourselves and still have accepted that within the content there is a message for you that will throw Light on the dark questioning areas of your being.

It is difficult to understand the avoidance of illumination, when all that is required is a willingness to seek a true answer for the question that has been raised. When you ask a question, it is assumed you require an answer. Now let us continue on the subject of Spirit evolvement. Many pass through life totally unaware of the existence of purpose and still manage to evolve, why and how? It is really simple to answer this question, easier to answer than to explain why more don't evolve further then they do, even though they have a greater awareness than most. To presume to know where you have decided your destiny is, is to enter the folly of pure belief. Those who enter the earth realm with the innocence of a child, retain that innocence in spite of all the pressures to conform to the system being imposed at that time, find that they have a purity that remains unspoiled and does not attach itself to the coarseness of materialism. These therefore do not have the added burden of detachment from the material and can live a life of greater harmony with the existence that they can then realise. They have the advantage of being able to live life to its fulfilment. They have the ability to live the experience in its proper way without struggle and to thus absorb that experience they seek without any trouble.

People on the earth normally find that which entices them from the easy route, generally on the promise of an easier life, only to find that life has incurred greater difficulties then they had been allowed to imagine. The benefits of an involvement with the material world are doubtful if this is the only promise that involvement would hold. Realise again that the earth exists only so that your Spirit may have the opportunity of finding itself in a state of experience that will be of spiritual benefit in assisting it back to God. Now why do we find that Spirits arriving into this the Spirit world are ill prepared for the awakening they receive? Is it a case of Spirit being wrong? Is it a case of they being wrong? No, it is simply that the coarseness of matter was found to be a more tangible reality then they could understand. Spirit was not wrong in any way, good or bad. The burden of responsibility for the evolvement of any Spirit lies with that Spirit itself. The Spirit has to even take responsibility for its own ignorance. In the present case of Spirit communication Spirit has taken the initiative to relay helpful information to those who wish to listen. There is no compulsion for any to listen. There is no condition put on any one to adopt the philosophy that is expounded. There is no removal of free will. It is the intention of Spirit that the information be given that will help mankind evolve, of its own free will, back to God. There can be no condition laid on any human by those who proclaim the sanctity of the Spirit and its right to become part of the great Illumination.

There are many in both worlds that would seek to impose their will on as many others as possible. These you must be aware of in order not to become subservient to a demigod. Many seek to set themselves up as such but that is their will, let it not be yours. We will go this night with these words, all was given to you so that you might experience the beauty and love that emanates from the Holy One, your Lord, Master of the Light, God.

COMMUNICATION.

It is necessary to attain the silence that is required for one to be in a position to perceive the slightest sound, for the utterances of Spirit are barely perceptible. This advice is given to you so that you may understand why it is that you do not receive or receive badly the communications from Spirit.

Many sit in judgement of the abilities of Spirit. It is not that difficult an act for Spirit to transmit a message to those on earth, it is those on earth that have the difficulty in receiving the message. In your world you have radio stations sending out signals but if you don't make the necessary arrangements to receive them, they go unnoticed by you, but they are nonetheless there. Many say they have not got the 'gift'; it is not a gift they require; they have the ability latent in their being but refuse to acknowledge this fact, refuse to spend the time learning how to acknowledge this fact. How many go to others (psychic mediums) for guidance and are given that which is really only relevant to the medium themselves, for it is how the medium sees the way things are for themselves. Facility can be made for those seekers to have their awareness developed further so that they may be in a clearer position to understand themselves and their own position in relation to the way things are for them in this their chosen life, without recourse to psychics. Do not lose sight of the fact that the life your life is, is as chosen by you and is for you to lead. Very often those indulging in acts of fortune telling or uncontrolled clairvoyance are just indulging in the emanations from their own misguided Soul and though given in all "honesty" by the giver very often are only misguidance to turn the recipient into a clone of the giver, no less enlightened, no greater evolved.

It is to give advice on the wrongful surrender of your own responsibilities that we talk as we do now. We do not seek to amaze you by the ability that is with the recipient of these writings. The manner in which these writings reach you are to allow you the choice of reading them or discarding them. You are not forced to read them but you are given the choice. If it were spoken words that you received then you would have to listen in order to make the decision whether to keep them or not, but then you have already chosen to listen in order to decide.

Do you understand that Spirit seeks to give you choice wherever possible? If you were to seek guidance from Spirit, Spirit would not make the choice for you but will certainly remove the confusion so that you are well aware which is the right choice for you to make. Spirit will never remove the facility of free will.

Remember this and be wary of those who seek to tell you what they feel Spirit has told them what you must do. Remember it is within the nature of humankind to seek the control of other human's lives so that they may be the testing grounds of the ideas the first human seeks to validate. If the idea does not pass the test then it is the guinea pig who suffers. No, my friends it is the wise who seek counsel with the wisely.

We are aware that there are those amongst you who seek to mislead you. They tell you of your guides, of your path, of your friends in Spirit. It would be well if you were perhaps to check the sources of the information these people receive. Very often they are themselves blind to their own deception of themselves. Many times we have spoken of ego poisoning, and here is one typical case. The folly of listening to these people is that the trap they are in has become the trap for you and they the bait. Very often they no longer know who they serve. They have all the words but that is all they are, words.

If you have read all that has been written up to these words you will have begun to recognise that there is a discernible personality behind them. If this is the case, then you are beginning to recognise true Spirit. You will notice that we never have a need to give a name so that you would recognise us. In this case we would have to give many names, Tom, Dick and Harry. But still you recognise this joint personality as one distinct personality. Do you not think this is wonderful of you? Realise also how you need have no reservations as to the source of these words for nobody can fool you for long into believing they are us, for you truly know us, and this is why we are friends. There are many who will try to imitate but it is your responsibility to be sufficiently discerning so as not to be fooled. Learn who and how to trust. Trust is a word that is often used to deceive, but yet trust must be allowed to be. How then do you know how to trust? There is one word, discernment. In Spirit communication this word, discernment is a valid one both on the earth plane and on the plane of Spirit.

There are many on the earth that seek to have your trust in order to deceive you. It is up to you to have discernment in order to have trust that you can trust. You must be able to trust yourself before you can truly trust others. There are many words that are very valid to the correct use in understanding. It is unfortunate that many more can also be added in order to disguise deceit. Let us talk more on this subject another day.

We have decided to bring these matters to your attention in order that you might be in a position that would be better suited to your evolvement; that you would better understand those who would try to mislead you from the truth; those who would seek to misguide you with words that you were not fully conversant with. We know that the path you trod is not the most obvious to you at this stage and it is at this stage that most effort will be made to draw you away from it.

There are many on both sides of the divide called death that would prefer it if you did not achieve enlightenment for it would help them to further justify their own predicament. We are from the one true Light of God and profess this openly in order that you may heed these words. There is not any need for this collective consciousness to attempt to deceive you, for it is in the furthering of your knowledge that you may have a greater concept of God and therefore will need less guidance to find your way along your path. We have no need for your thanks, we have no need for your opinions to be gratifying. We have need of your love and we have need of your company for is it not in the completion of the Godhead that all becomes one, that total harmony can exist and God can be in all Glory. You are a part in this unity. It is for you to return.

May God include you in His Blessings.

COMPROMISE.

It is with a compromise that we approach you this night. Compromise is a very dangerous solution to any difference; however, we do not see it in this instance to be so. What is in mind is to assist you in the understanding of goals in life.

It is necessary that some basis be formed that will enable us to discuss the imponderable without the discussion forming a basis for misunderstanding. We have lived in an existence on earth and have still knowledge of the level of understanding that is available in that state. Our recollection is a little hazy and we find that we tend to allow ourselves too much freedom in our imparting some of our knowledge to you, thereby causing some confusion.

The compromise we talk of therefore, is that we all allow some facility for understanding within our own limitations and still allow the conjecture that will permit the final truth to only emerge later. Now, it is a classical situation in that the teacher is in possession of more knowledge than the pupil, yet the pupil always manages to impart knowledge to the teacher, this is why all-around openness is necessary for we also need to learn from you. So, let us proceed.

This night we will talk on ignorance. It is ignorant to reject the facility for gaining wisdom. To say, therefore, that most of mankind is ignorant would not be too much of an exaggeration. You might find this suggestion repugnant, yet in doing so you prove the point we make. Surely it would have been wise to have listened further so that you might understand better the statement before you rejected it? Now you see the need for compromise in this situation. Let us proceed, that you do reject so much of that which is given leaves you in that state of ignorance that leaves you so vulnerable to the denizens of the darker areas of total existence. Your ignorance is such that you do not permit yourself the opportunity to learn more of the life you lead, of the true purpose of that life, of the true significance of the existence of the facility for learning the answers that continuously upset the thinking of mankind. We may appear harsh at times yet if you were to allow yourself full facility of your intellect together with the honest openness then all illumination would be received.

There are many lessons we receive from your deliberations; many is the memory that is evoked for us. It is a constant striving for understanding that keeps us searching for ways that we may understand that which precedes us, and it is the knowledge that we gain in this search that we impart to you. It happens that we find from time to time a contradiction in our thinking due to fresh enlightenment, and thus we have to revise our thoughts and transmit these changes to you.

This situation causes you confusion but it need not. In the science of research, it is necessary that the openness we talked of earlier is maintained for it is only then that progress can be made. If the question were stifled before the answer was forthcoming then no understanding could ever be achieved. Understand that the search for knowledge is ever dynamic in that it is only by attaining a certain level of understanding that another level can be achieved and ignorance left behind.

Many are they that thrive on ignorance in that they use it as an excuse to avoid truth, the truth that they are refusing to be enlightened. Many hide in the darkness never to venture into the light, and this is why we are so readily available to be of assistance to any who might seek to carry the Light into their darkness. You will notice as you travel your path that you will encounter many who are seeking, many who have a conditional seeking.

There are many who only seek confirmation of their own ignorance and rest happy when they receive it. We say to these, yes, this is your truth rest happy with it, if you can, do not let the complications of knowledge knock you from your perch. Yes, rest happy while you can for it will not last long before you realise that the rest has brought you to your demise, then there will be the rush to scramble back to reality so as to avoid being washed over the waterfall. Again, harsh words but none the less true words.

Remember the compromise and allow yourself the facility to gain the knowledge that will allow you to understand these words. So, we have spoken of ignorance at length but yet not enough. Apply these words every time you feel the need to reject something that might give you wisdom, and perhaps you may learn more. Again, these words are given in love as are the many signs that God is very much accessible to mankind for it is the Love of God that enables us to be in a position to reject or accept these teachings that come to you. We ask that you in your turn accept them from us. May God Bless you all with the wisdom to accept and understand all that is given in His name.

DEATH.

My friends it is inevitable that the day must dawn when nothing more can be done on this earth. Yes, it is death that we speak of, for it is important that you have an understanding of this the ultimate act on the earth plane.

The necessity of death is to enable the incarnated Spirit to find the release from the imprisonment of the physical body and to ascend into the higher realms of spirituality. There is no other way that this can be achieved. We may look to the bible so as to illustrate this. To end the story of Jesus it was necessary that he be allowed to die, thereby bringing to an end that phase of his life and allowing him to enter the new life that was waiting for him. He did not fear this transition any more or less than any other man, "Father, Father why hast thou forsaken me?" he cried. This was not the plea from one who was totally committed to his fate. No, this was the manifestation of the apprehension experienced facing the unknown. It is also the ultimate opportunity to test one's faith, in that if there is this trust then that trust will extend even then, into the apparent darkness of death. Only then can one experience the beauty that can unfold without the shadows of fear dimming the sight of the beholder.

Death of the physical body is perhaps more normal than the birth. It is more normal to die having lived than to be born. Death does not affect the Spirit. It does not cause any discomfort to that part of the being. Death only affects the physical body. How many times does one surrender the body to the effects of an influence such as alcohol, drugs, whether medicinal or not, or some such other sense suspending intoxicant? How often do you as an individual meditate? In meditation you seek the temporary separation of the Spirit from the body. Death is no different.

An observer may define it differently, however. Their view is influenced by the resistance of the body to the changes taking place. You often hear reference to the quality of a person's death, they had a violent death, a painful death, a peaceful death, the factors relating to these conditions are purely physical.

There is no pain in death, the Spirit cannot feel pain of a physical nature. The body might be subjected to violence but the Spirit is immune to the physical nature of this experience. There can be great peace in that the experience is understood, and a great sense of relief is experienced. The Spirit can leave uninhibited. Surely this latter experience is the end that most would seek, an end where all is as one in peace love and harmony? Again, let us remind you that this peace love and harmony is but an experience gained through a knowledge of oneself, one's position, and one's perception of God and the unification of all this knowledge in the closeness of God Knowing. All has been achieved that can possibly be achieved and eternity now presents you with a seat closer to your destination, God.

So this is death, this is what is so often feared, how do you feel now? Another factor that causes much discomfort in passing from the material world is the material well-being that remains after your demise. Very often the accumulation of this material wealth has been in a manner that can only be described as selfish, a need to have more than another, greed. The folly of indulgence in this manner is that the dying vision you will experience will be the divisions of your remains, your accumulated material wealth, remember Jesus on the cross and the dice players vying for his cloak.

If on the other hand you have spent a life of sharing and caring then you will have an attitude of giving and not resent the redistribution of your goods. You can see now how the quality of your living can reflect on the quality of your dying, as you live so shall you die. There are many different ways that you can live and die, and many different ways that you can attempt resisting death.

Let not your self be fooled into thinking that you can prolong your physical life beyond its end, you cannot, when it is time for the end there it will be, just be prepared and then it will always be the right time. But, realise that death is not the end of the Spirit, no, it is only to release the Spirit. You were always Spirit and always will be Spirit. It is not the end of Spirit. Remember that Spirit is energy and a scientific fact of your earth physics is that energy cannot be created nor destroyed, this is true, therefore Spirit cannot be created nor destroyed, but it can continue to exist in another form. So, you see there is not any reason to fear death by the act of dying alone, however, if one has reason then there can be fear, resentment and reluctance to face the inevitable. These latter are all physical conditions and you must understand of your own creation. By your own power you can change these conditions and allow yourself the luxury of enjoying death.

Release yourself from this fear and live your life as it is meant to be lived, looking towards to successful completion of your period of earth incarnation and then you can truly rest in peace, after a job well done. Go now in God's Light.

PERFECT FOR THE JOB.

My friends it is with a certain joy in our hearts that we gather this evening. Many have come to this place and many have gone from this place yet this place still is. From this you will understand that this is not a place of permanency rather a place to receive that which is needed and to then move on. There is no need to feel tied to here as this place is only a place.

Many have felt the need to remove themselves so as to maintain movement and then have felt the need to return for further enlightenment only to find that they have misunderstood their original motive for removing themselves in the first place. Understand that these doors are always open to those in need and should you find yourself in the position of being nowhere then you may find your way here and be someplace. We have felt the need to bring this point to everyone's attention for we observe that there are those that have begun a new seeking and have need of this place. You must allow them to understand that they are welcome to return. Their return is our joy.

Now we will continue. Many times now we have spoken of the weaknesses that encroach on the being that is known as humankind, this weak vessel for the Spirit. You may wonder why such an imperfect thing such as a human being could be created by such perfection that is God. Many times, you have felt that the fault lay with God and the reason why you were imperfect was because you were made that way. Realise this that the human being is in itself perfect for the task it has to fulfil, the bringing of the Spirit into contact with that which it needs to learn or experience. You will notice that we have separated the words learn and experience, the reason for this is to enable you to understand that not every experience is a learning one, nor every lesson an experience.

Let us continue, we therefore illustrate our qualification of the human being as being perfect by suggesting that you take a good long look at yourself and understand that you got what you asked for. Next take a good long look at yourself and try and see why you have what you have. On the hypothesis that what you have is perfect then understand therefore there is a definite function for your being as you are. If you can approach yourself with all honesty then you should have no difficulty in understanding your true purpose. The only difficulty is that you cannot approach yourself in all honesty. You might find this statement inaccurate; then why do you so often need others to tell you your purpose, your path, your next move? Only because you cannot be totally honest with yourself.

It is hoped that now you will begin to understand that the human being you are was given to you in a state of perfection that would enable you to fulfil the function of this incarnation, that you will understand that the function of this body is to allow you to find the imperfection that you have in your Spirit and then provide you with the facility to illuminate as many of these imperfections as you set out from the heavens to illuminate. Feel free to take as much time as you need to do this task for that is the time, the only time there is, in the Spirit concept.

The fact that you realise too much time has been taken is only an illustration of how close you operate within the confines of the physical cycle that is only to do with your humanism. You will always have sufficient time to fulfil your purpose as long as you consciously seek to fulfil it. Many find that they spend too much time in serving the temporal needs of the body, which is a time-consuming occupation, instead of giving the short time, that earth life is, to maximising the opportunity of spiritual evolvement. See to it that the time you have in the flesh is spent wisely and then you will find that much time is available to pander to the body also.

The body deserves respect, it is a living thing, it feels, it tastes and does all the things that enables the Spirit to assimilate the necessary lessons that are to be learned on the earth plane. Give that body respect but do not spoil it.

Might we leave you these few words to-night, let those who seek know they are welcome in this place, let those who wish to return, return, let those who wish to know about perfection hark to these words. The fault is in you, in your very being, in your Spirit, and you are going about improving your understanding in order to improve your essence, your Spirit, so that you may begin to grow towards the Most Supreme. It is only by increasing your illumination that you may ultimately blend into that which is the brightest, God. May God bestow His greatest blessings upon you. Go in peace and understanding.

SEARCH FOR THE SELF.

Many times we have spoken of the `mysteries' of the Spirit world and many times we have sought to help you understand how to attain these realms. The world of Spirit is readily attainable by all for it is the natural progression from that world you presently inhabit. You have no choice in the matter for your commitment to the will of the Almighty One made it necessary that you fully understand all that there is to know.

We know you will question the free will in the context that it has, in this instance, been ignored but listen to these words; we speak to the flesh not the Spirit when we address you as we do now. Therefore you, as a Spirit being, have given yourself to the will of God so that you might attain the highest that is for you to attain. We of course speak of total evolvement.

Many times we have spoken of the Spirit world in that we have spoken of God for that is where He dwells. One must realise that to enter this world is not unusual, it is perfectly normal for it is your real home. To enter it through the door of death is also normal for the time that you wish to return for a longer period.

You see that to enter this realm and stay too long while still in the flesh would starve the flesh of the necessary energy to stay alive and therefore render the body useless to the Spirit on its return.

One must also be aware that to dwell too long in meditation is not necessarily good for the body either, for the same principle applies in that the body is exhausted through the draining of the vital energy. This draining might give the participant in the meditation a certain euphoria, but then so can bloodletting and that is not necessarily always good for one. Let us see then the purpose of meditation and as to its validity in the search for the inner or the outer self. This elusive self dwells in the body of humankind whilst it is in an earth incarnation. There is no validity in searching for it in the Spirit realms, therefore you must seek it within. The purpose of accessing these realms is only valid in that you expand your own consciousness and can therefore have a greater awareness of that which you seek. In meditation you often excitedly seek to explore the outer reaches, the far horizons of the Spirit world. This is not a valid pursuit if it is yourself that you seek. If you seek your self, look to yourself. The meditation you take that takes you into the cavern is one such valid journey.

The journey to meet with your guardian is also valid, let this be your chaperon. The meditation where you wash is valid in that you must cleanse yourself of the negativity that you have taken into yourself during your stay on that earth. The structure of the meditations you have experienced have been to clean and heal, to give you a glimpse into this reality so that you may feel more prepared to take the journey into your own spirituality. This journey is not to be daunting. Provision has been made to give you the strength that is necessary to venture into those areas that were hitherto unknown to the self that seeks to explore them. In the exploration of this world, you will find that all is not unfamiliar, even your guide is not unfamiliar. Your guide may be a stranger but not unfamiliar. If you were to find all you experience in this world unfamiliar, you would not find it acceptable. Therefore, this would, to some extent, be a reasonable reaction. We suggest that you take the time to feel if this is the case, if you do not feel at home in your meditation.

If you experience a reaction that gives you a negative reaction then we would suggest that you seek to understand your motivation in meditating in the first place. Meditation is only meant to be a positive experience. When next you meditate remember these words. There is nothing too complicated in the search for the self, the only complication is in the acceptance of that which you present to yourself. It is not nice to find that the being you think you are is not in fact who you are. Primarily you are a Spirit of a beauty that is incomprehensible. At this stage you may appear a little tarnished but realise that in successive reincarnations, whether through the earth plane or otherwise you have managed to brighten little by little.

You can be pleased with your progress for all is then coming to right. Many have taken to the path of return and yet some struggle in their ignorance, even now in the stage you are at, ignorance is such an inhibiting factor. You struggle and struggle using the same knowledge to try to lift yourself from the state of ignorance that you still find yourself in.

Notice we have stressed that you have used the same criterion to try to lift yourself. You must realise that it is only by gaining fresh knowledge that a fresh start can be made in trying to reach higher levels of understanding. Be aware that a higher level of understanding can only be reached by going to those with a higher knowledge. Therefore, you must meditate for this also. Having found your self you can then find the level of the self-understanding and through further meditation seek to bring that level of understanding higher and higher. It is necessary then that you venture beyond the self, beyond the earth world, out, out into the outer realms out into the realms of Spirit, to read your book of knowledge, to use your key to the many rooms that contain the wisdom that you seek, to firmly plant yourself in the garden of paradise.

Seek not to glorify this excursion for it was not designed as a task of glorification; seek not to take only the niceties from the realisation of the self. Realise that, that which is within that physical body though internally beautiful has a much-scarred surface, that it needs to be resurfaced, that it needs to be polished. You are far from perfect as we too are not yet perfect but must also seek to understand where we are on this evolutionary scale.

Bear with us, be with us so that our joint seeking may prove infinitely more fruitful, for the pool of knowledge is deeper for the amount of spirituality we can then gather about all ourselves. We leave you now to ponder. Even meditate on these words and we await your call for us to join with you and you join with us in this glorious migration back to God.

May He bless us all in our endeavours.

TIME.

It is in this instant that creation of thought emerges. This opening statement is to allow you the facility to understand that thought is instantaneous. Why is it that we wish you to have this understanding? So that you realise the closeness that is you and us. We are only a thought away from your world yet that distance is measurable, measurable in terms that you can understand, a thought away, yet instant.

Again we return to time concepts, we have no time, you have time. You occupy a dimensional world, it has length, breath, height, all easily acceptable in terms that you can perceive. We live in a multidimensional world and still there is no means of measuring, no time, no distance, no height. Do you begin to feel what this is like? Read this again, and again if necessary, until you begin to feel this limitless existence. Yes, all limitations are in your existence and you have the tendency to make more limitations. How often do you say that you cannot do something yet there is no real reason for the statement if you really have the desire to do it? No, you impose all limitations on yourself by your own desire to avoid that which you deem to be an effort in endeavour. You by your will limit your meditation, your evolvement, your progress towards eternity. Yes, we do rebuke you for this idleness that you permit, that you allow to develop in your being and thus negate all progress. We know that it is all humankind that we address with these statements for all humankind are guilty of this malaise. We do realise that this is just part of the imperfection that is human, yet we are not prepared to allow you the facility of self-indulgence in such a negative form. Again, we stress that you impose limitations on your being that do not justify acknowledgement.

Now to tell of other things. We have been critical of the behaviour of humankind. This criticism is to be in the nature of knowledge not of the nature of total rebuke. No, we do not seek to stifle any movement you might seek to make, rather to encourage you to move for then you can journey to your destination. You must realise that for you to again limit yourself, by imposing limitations of movement on yourself, would be counterproductive on the meaning of this communication. Do not stop rather be careful of the road you take.

When flesh first was devised it was the intention that this vehicle would be the carrier of the Spirit throughout its lifetimes in the earth world. Later it was discovered that indeed this was not fully right, for it was necessary that a certain independence was needed by the physical so that it too could develop into the vehicle that was required by the evolving Spirit. To maintain this dynamism, it was therefore implanted with the dynamism we speak of and this is where the vulnerability of the flesh can overtake the evolvement of the Spirit. Because the Spirit is so dependent on the flesh to take it where it needs to go it is obvious that the Spirit must be better recognised so that it may be taken to the correct destination. Many times there is a complete lack of understanding of the need of the Spirit and consequently the Spirit never reaches where it seeks to go.

Humankind has this commitment to its Spirit and the sooner it realises this it can then find a greater harmony in its life. Seek not for flesh fulfilment, rather seek to satisfy the Spirit through the flesh. We feel that this explanation of the paradox of the words "being made flesh" is good in illustrating the 'topsy-turvey' world that has been evolved to satisfy the flesh especially with so little recognition of the Spirit involved. Seek to first to find the Spirit within and next to relate this Spirit being with the self you now recognise, combine the two and you have the right combination for successful evolvement.

We will leave you now to ponder these words as we realise that we have in fact imposed a burden on you that did not exist until now. We have spoken of the incomprehensible in comprehensible terms and hope that you will give these few lines sufficient study to enable yourself to become fully familiar with what has been said. It is a duty you have to yourself. You seek to know, therefore you shall, for this is the promise of the Great One, The True Light, the only God.

May this God bless us with the facility to assimilate all wisdom.

RATIONALISATION.

When much is found that is distasteful to your thought then the inclination is for you to discount it. It is on this topic that we would concentrate this time. Discounted thought, - many feel that they have the control on their lives and for us to show them otherwise would lead them to discount the notion that the idea they had of themselves is less then accurate.

When humankind was first evolved, it was for this purpose that conflict of thought was permitted to be retained, for it invoked rationalisation. Rationalisation is a process whereby humankind can find out for itself if the thoughts it has are in fact valid to the thinking it feels is appropriate to its own understanding and also to its life. It is unfortunate that mainly it is thought for life that is allowed to dominate the thinking and therefore an unbalanced rationalisation occurs. Now if a clearer understanding of life were gained first then perhaps it would not be so. Humankind tends to rush for the top whilst ignoring the subtleties that exist along the way. In this fashion humankind arrives at the early conclusion that life is living a physical existence and there is only a duty to live it to the physical full. This is not the case; life is a physical existence enshrining the Spirit so that the Spirit can maintain a facility on the earth whereby it may obtain all the experiences that this particular life has to give.

It is again unfortunate that greater Spirit awareness is not gained through the normal channels of learning, for the Spirit knows what it is but the body still needs to learn that it is not the purpose for this life and to learn what it is that dwells inside of it. Much needs to be done, indeed undone in this area.

We have spent many generations of earth existence ourselves attempting to solve the situation only to find that we too, in that existence, had become its victim and succumbed to the temptations that were laid in our paths. We too refuted the knowledge that was presented to us. We too took excessive time on the earth trying to evolve the body and neglected the Spirit. The journey could have been faster had we but understood the intricacies of evolvement. Now it is all too easy to see where we went wrong and the pitfalls we fell into. We come to you to warn you of the follies you will entertain to your own detriment. We see now that many seek to only evolve the human race, to make it superior, to draw away from its nature, to be super-beings. How can this be so if the Spirit is neglected? Remember that the balance has to be maintained, that the Spirit has to balance with the body, with the mind. Remember that all has to be in harmony. Remember that without the Spirit the body is nothing, it is dead. Remember by suppressing the Spirit into almost insignificance is to draw the body close to death. Remember that to die thus is suicidal. These are thoughts that you may wish to rationalise out of existence but yet you cannot, for having been told you must listen in some way and to have done that little listening you have allowed the thought to penetrate somewhere into the consciousness, planting the seed that must someday rise to the surface to again be faced even though it may be in the light of another understanding.

You see now why it is better to address the situation openly when it occurs, seeking the understanding that will enable you to correctly assimilate the knowledge to be gained, sooner than casting out the thought unthinkingly. We will leave you these words to ponder and while you ponder on these words do not forget the way that you treated other words that were also given for your illumination at other times. Maybe you might even turn to them again, face them again in the light of this new understanding.

Go now with God's blessing to ponder on all words, selflessly given, for the illumination of the thinking of all humankind.

THE FANTASY LAND.

Many have come before to illustrate that area known as the Spirit world. As a little holiday from the drudgery of intense teaching, where the mind and imagination are being continuously attacked by thoughts that were hitherto unthought-of, we shall now enter into a land of fantasy.

You will know from earlier communications that we have spoken in practical terms of the world of Spirit and now, though we use the term fantasy, we do not intend to impart the idea that this world is unreal. Rather we want you to understand that this world is so real that it is difficult to comprehend in your terms, a fantasy land. If we were to take you on the briefest excursion it would need a book of vast proportions to record in any detail any of the wonderful sights that are here to behold. As this world is constructed by Spirit for Spirit there are many levels, many dimensions. We have spoken before of being multidimensional. You must understand that to you there are yet many dimensions that you have not the capacity to comprehend. An example of this is in relation to your world, how many actually can see a Spirit, not many, yet some can. Your immediate reaction to this not seeing is that as you can't see therefore it isn't. But this is not true, many can see Spirit and therefore it is. The same reasoning is also prevalent with regard to this place, as it cannot be seen therefore it isn't. You meditate, you see, but it must be imagination, but in truth you must know that you cannot imagine in that detail. Why then do you not accept that here exists, we are here. And so too is this fantasy we talked about, only to us it is reality.

Glorious beholding of all glory that is a reality only to be beheld by those whose acceptance of this word, will open to this glory, and in doing so share in the glory that is intended for all humankind one day to behold. Make that day this day.

We intend this day to expose you to this reality. It is your choice whether to accept or not. Many have walked this path before as indeed you have also. To understand that this is the eternal land is to accept the philosophy of all knowing, of understanding that all is there to be known, and to seek to gain that knowledge that is for all. It is impossible that all will manage to understand all in this short dissertation, but yet a seed will be planted that will enable all to access the enlightenment that will be needed to broaden the facility of perception, so as to eventually encompass all that is to be understood. When first you enter this land, you will see very little to differentiate this land from the land you have just left. Initially you will seek to identify with here through comparison with there. Slowly at first you will notice that all is not as it first seems, even though there are definite similarities. There are many lands like on your earth. There is much vegetation as on your earth. There are many animals as on your earth. There are many races as on your earth. All this is only because you cannot yet see other than you are used to, or you see only that which you are prepared to accept. Would you for instance accept a sabre-toothed tiger were you to meet one? No, you would not want to meet one of those, so therefore you shan't. You see this is a world that only is as tangible as you need it to be.

It is not too different from your earth world in that you can limit your capacity for vision in the earth dimension also. How often do you only see that which you want to see and never see that which you need to see? Often we endeavour to expand your consciousness by producing some phenomena, but then you allow yourself to over indulge to the extent that it is no longer valid as a phenomenon, but is only entertaining. And then you wonder why the phenomena stops. However, back to this world, here too there are many wonders to stimulate the imagination and to thus open the mind to the seeing and acceptance of matters that are of the utmost importance to the evolving Spirit.

Here too you have choice. You may choose to allow these wonders to become commonplace, never to utilise them for the expansion of your own thought, so as you may gain that extra grasp on this ever-new reality. How often in that world of yours do you fail to look much higher than the level of your own eyes, the level of your own understanding, never seeking for anything higher? All to often you deny yourself this facility and so too when you first come here, you tend to continue this practice. There, as here you need to adopt the attitude that there is a need to seek higher views on all aspects, if you get the ability to this perception whilst still on that level then you will find it of great assistance on this level. You will then be able to have greater capacity to assimilate the vibration of this world and to see more of that which is to be seen, and to permit yourself facility for greater expansion of your spiritual consciousness.

There is not much more to add to the many tomes that have already been written about this plane. Many have been the stories used to illustrate the way things are or could be whilst in Spirit. There is no need for us to add a repetition to the many words already given, for that would serve no great purpose. Rather we would say to you to be aware of that which has been written. If you find that you then have a greater capacity for more concepts, then we can accommodate you in transcribing more for you. You will find however, that on reaching that stage you will also realise that you have not yet reached the level where you can look for more, rather like walking on a hill, when you think you have reached the summit you find that it is still there to be conquered.

Don't forget there is an eternity of knowledge to be gained and yet you only occupy an immeasurable portion of that eternity. How then do you expect to be able to understand all regarding here, from there? We would suggest that you ponder on these words more before you seek further. Then perhaps you will shake off some of the dust that clouds your thinking, and allow yourself a fresh look at that which you think you already know. This should occupy you for the rest of that living before you need to take a closer look at this world. Perhaps then you will be in a better position to understand that which you will see, and be aware of that you cannot see.

We find that the ability to fantasise a most welcome ability, for then we can imprint fantastic impressions on the mind during practises such as meditation. Do not condemn images as flights of fantasy, for often you are not believing that which you have just been given for your illumination.

We will leave you now so that you may set aside the time to open your mind to us, your friends in Spirit, your Spirit friends. Open your mind so that you may gain knowledge, so that you allow the Light to enter, so that you may understand. The languages of humankind are restrictive to Spirit, for none of them contain sufficient words to encompass all that needs description so as to satisfy the wants of humankind. There are however sufficient to satisfy the needs of the human.

So, we have spoken of this place some more and have left you still with more questions. We have sought to bring you an understanding of that which is really not yet to be understood, and have yet suggested trains of thought which will enable you to attain a certain understanding within the parameters of the capacity of the earth bound human-being. This is indeed to you a fantasy land. We leave you now in the quandary that is the physical world. We do not leave you without our love and the earnest wish that you may achieve the goals you have set for you to attain. Go now in peace and love. Go in God's Light.

HOPE (2).

My friends it is with hope that we come this evening, hope that these words will be received in the manner in which they are given. These words are for the enlightenment of mankind. They are not meant to confuse or to provoke negative reaction. No, these words are given in the spirit of giving, given unconditionally for those who entertain a true wish to find answers to their questions.

We spoke the last time about the difficulties of comprehending the Spirit world and of the limitations imposed by the human consciousness. This is a lingering difficulty that has to be tolerated in-so-far as humankind in its seeking can only expand its consciousness at a very slow rate. It is difficult for you to understand the enormity of the task you face when you step onto the road to God, however, your lack of comprehension is also the factor that assists you for if you were to know, then the prospect would possibly appear too daunting.

It is inevitable that you will arrive at your destination sometime, as the necessity for the total completion of the perfection requires it to be perfect. As you are an integral part of that perfection - though at present you are far from that perfection - it would be incomplete without you. So you see that the heavenly gates cannot close until all return.

Now, at this time there are many who have already entered this world and frequently they return to your world as Spirit, to help you understand the direction you seek to go. If you had not got the perception to receive these personages then you would not have arrived to where you are. We do not speak of your guides in this instance. Those of whom we speak are from those higher realms and it is by your awareness of their existence, that you can get that little glimpse of the further reaches of this Spirit world. If you were to ignore their presence you would not have the perception to give you the momentum to move towards them. It is like a magnetic attraction that you feel, imperceptible to the physical being because of its coarseness, but infinitely perceptible to the Spirit. It is the love of God that becomes the prime mover of all Spirit in its migration back to their home, to their oneness.

We shall now speak on other matters. As we have just seen there are many forces acting on your behalf and as yet you move at so slow a pace. Why is this? We have drawn your attention to the fact that the action of these forces acts on the Spirit and not on the physical. Therefore, it is obvious that those who concentrate their energies on the physical would have the tendency to live their life unaware of the existence of these aids to their evolvement.

It is essential that an awareness of these forces is obtained. You ask how this can be done and the answer is simple, though the action of these forces may be quite elusive. The simplicity makes it difficult, for logic used against such subtly leaves very little space for understanding of these forces. To fully understand these forces, one must allow themselves to experience them rather than to attempt to rationalise them. To attempt to rationalise them would render the subtleness void, and therefore no understanding could be gained. For a clearer understanding to be gained it is necessary that a supposition is allowed, and, that you allow that which is subtle to become more obvious, and thus strengthen your own ability to perceive. In this way you will permit yourself to gain sufficient knowledge to then enter unto a path that is more exploratory and understandable. Then you may risk the application of logic to your thinking so that you may develop an intellectual outlook, and consequently a more acceptable format for expression to your fellow men. Your fellow men in their turn will also have to undergo a similar experience before they can begin to understand anything at all, in truth.

Intellectualising, on that which you know little, appears to be a habit often indulged in by those who lack a degree of spiritual insight. Spirit is never intellectual, therefore cannot be found in these quarters. Spirit may intellectualise in order to gain access to the mind that behaves in that manner. Truth can never exist in the hypothesis of intellectual power. Seek not the truth in the obscurity of the intellect. The truth is never hidden deep. It is the ignorance of the seeker that builds the barriers that have to be overcome before the truth can be seen.

You will understand that it is your own ignorance that you have to overcome, it is your own reluctance to understand the simplicity. It is this simplicity that shields the truth from the minds of men, through their own ignorance.

We will go now to allow you the time to unravel the truth from these words. The simple truth is that you seek to return to God, yet these simple words are not sufficient to allow you to see that this is all you really seek. Therefore, you must undergo successive rebirths into the physical world, experience great deprivation, suffer mental disturbance, tax that poor body in such hard and complicated ways, only to arrive at an understanding of these simple words, God is all there is, and that is what you are part of.

Go now in His Love and with his blessing.

THE ANTI-CHRIST.

My friends it is time that the activities of the anti-Christ were curtailed. This is no idle request for it is within your ability to do so. Everyone has in them an aspect of this power and this is the portion that needs elimination. We talk of Spirit in positive terms but only in so far as you might need to be more positively enlightened.

In this instance we seek to increase your awareness of that which lurks within the being of every human being, the anti-Christ. It is important, equally important that this aspect is looked at and understood for if you were to remain in ignorance of its existence, then, you would only then become its victim. When you fell from that which is most holy, most high, it was not through disfavour. You sought to become the wholeness, not a part of that wholeness. You sought the power that would entail the destruction of innumerable parts, for the power is contained in each part and for you to have more than is for you, meant that you would take the very life force from other parts, thereby destroying them. This is the anti-Christ, this is that part that has a need for exposition, and then elimination.

When you read this, you will probably feel an abhorrence at the suggestion that within you is the capacity to hold this intense negativity, you are not alone. It is the collective power of many seeking to use this negativity, that brings forth the phenomena that is generally termed witchcraft. There is no place in positive evolvement for any portion of this power. So that you may progress, it is necessary that you shed this aspect, but how? First it must be sought out, then isolated, then, when you are satisfied that you are fully aware of its many existences, you may change its form through transmutation, that is change it into good. As this is an energy that we speak of then treat it as such. Many energies in this system that you occupy are altered for the good, you can harness the force of the wind to generate good power that is useful to humankind. So too with this energy you can transform it into a useful form, for the benefit of your fellow humans.

You cannot destroy it, for it is indestructible. You cannot pack it away for another day, that is what has been done with it already. No, on discovery you must eliminate it once and for all. We have spoken already of the potency of this evil, it is so strong that it has brought you to the stage you were at, lost. Now you have found yourself, you must keep going.

The negativity we speak of can become manifest at any time. We have spoken before of the negative emotions and yet again we must refer to them for it is through these emotions that this insidiousness works, hate, jealousy, greed, and all other negative emotions including most of all ego. When ego strikes then all emotions can become tainted and diseased. When other emotions are allowed to dominate, they do not have such a negative effect as ego, though if they are one of the negative forms, then no matter how trivial an outburst is released, untold weakening takes place. Ego is by far the most destructive emotion that is within the human, perhaps the greatest manifestation of the anti-Christ. We seek to help you in all aspects of your evolvement, but this is one area that we cannot actively participate in. This is up to you alone to conquer; we can only advise you. Do not give any credence to those negative emotions stirring within you, for they seek your destruction. As you step away from them so their power over you lessens, yet they still exert power against you.

We will leave you now with this awareness and ask that you examine these aspects of your being. When this awareness is gained, then perhaps you will consider your next move in relation to eliminating them. If you wish you may question further and we would suggest that you ask for the strength to overcome this nature that is within you. Meditation is considered as a positive exercise to gain this strength. Above all the best weapon in this battle is wisdom, for then you will know how to be one with God, with no place for negativity to exist. Go in His love.

MULTIDIMENSIONAL KNOWLEDGE.

This time is no different to any other. Any differences that might appear to be, occur outside the confines of time. These words might seem strange but as we have already explained it is necessary to perceive a dimension outside of the generally accepted limitations. The outcome of this understanding will be access to universal knowledge, knowledge outside the limitations of humankind, esoteric knowledge. This is multidimensional knowledge.

We say that the limitations confine us too, for we have to work within your limitations. Let us continue about change, much has changed since we began this communication. Not just in terms of time, for that is irrelevant, but in terms of understanding.

Think back through the successive communications that have been sent. Read one or two again. What appeared hard to understand now appears totally simple. How could you have failed to understand in the first place? Now you see how things have changed.

The measurement that Spirit uses, is the distance between the essence of their being, God, and themselves. Even this distance is not as your measurement but could perhaps be likened to your gravity; in that the further you distance yourself from the source of the pull, the lesser is the strength of attraction. Take your present position, if you like we are closer to God than you are; therefore, there is a greater attraction for us than for you. As you become more spiritual, so the closer you get to God; therefore, the task gets easier. It is all a question of your position.

Now we look into the speed of your return. If you keep on your path, then you will find an acceleration along it as the drag on you diminishes. This drag is doubt, this drag is ignorance. As you release these drags then you accelerate along your path, becoming more susceptible to the pull, the attraction of God.

So now we have changed your perception yet again. There are many instances of your understanding being based on the measurements imposed by the physical life that you need to experience, yet in the sense of Spirit these measurements have no bearing. Steps cannot be taken on your spiritual path until the time is right. There it is again, time. But this time we speak of, is not measurable by any clock, no it is measured by your understanding. It is rather like these words. We spoke already about the changes that have taken place. These words are not fully understood until you have the ability to understand them. If you understand them now, it is only because it is the time, no hours, days, months or years, the time is only now.

Let us expose yet another misnomer, now. The only time is now, for now was then, now will be now, now is now. There is no time like now, how true that statement is. In preparation of this now, realise that you are not creating time you are just being aware of the now. When you decide to take a particular action then the decision is always referred to the consequences of your time, which is no time in reality. Therefore, when next you decide to plan be aware of the nature of your plan, if it is of a physical nature then it is deserving of physical time, and if it is of a spiritual nature then it is deserving of spiritual time, the now.

Go now in time, your time, time will tell. Live in the now time and there is no telling, only living. You are a being, therefore be. We hope that you will unravel this knowledge, for until you do it will not be knowledge, but it will in time, the right time. Go in peace, love and harmony, for there are those who have love for you and await your awakening to their existence.

Go in God's love and with His blessing.

JOURNEY INTO THE SPIRIT WORLD.

It is strange to say that all that has been spoken in these writings has gone beyond the normal ability of human comprehension, yet, if you still understand these words. This is indicative of the expansion of your own consciousness. When we speak now you find a greater truth in these words, and that is how it should be.

This time we shall speak of the world of Spirit once again. Go now into that state that allows you to access better the understanding that we need so as to impart this knowledge to you. Go now into a state of relaxation with the consciousness barely intruding into this state. We need the consciousness to be active so that it may transmit the signals into the deeper reaches of the human mind and from there allow the process to be completed by its assimilation into the very Spirit. These words are for the Spirit so that it can strengthen sufficiently to overcome the strong physical presence that has been allowed to accumulate. Go into this state, allow a pause at this stage, relax. Wait..........

This world is like no other. There are many worlds, many levels of existence in these worlds but none like it is here. Why? This is the world of the Spirit that is why. Other worlds have in their own way a need for a "physical" vehicle of sorts so as to allow the Spirit to be transported about the realm of existence that is for the Spirit to experience. When you venture out of your world you too don a uniform that permits you to survive the state of the world that you have entered into. So too it is here, for you to enter this realm you have need to have the facility for survival.

There is no need for the physical body, it would not exist here except as an imaginary form. There would be no real substance in the form. While here you must be in the mental state that requires no physical form. When you meditate you allow your mind to travel into this realm. Your mind allows your Spirit to be transported with it into the home of Spirit. There is a reason for this action for as the Spirit is linked into the mind in this instance then when the mind wishes to return to its own world, your present world, the Spirit has to follow. Thus, you cannot stay here until it is your time to complete your earth incarnation.

Many travel here in meditation and find that it is so much like the world they have just left, or, that it is the wonderland they have dreamed of, and so on, this is just the limitations of their own understanding that are being expressed. Do not be alarmed by this observation as this is what we need to illustrate. Imagination plays a large part in the tableau that can unfold to you when you visit here. Realise this and be thankful that you have this facility but remember that you have yet to go further and do not allow yourself the complacent attitude that you have arrived at your destination and remain stuck in that state until you realise that there is still a long way to go.

We have already described the preliminary stages that are experienced on entering into this realm. When you have overcome the initial trials of a new-born then, like in your existence there, you can begin to continue your journey into this world. Don't forget that you have to refresh yourself before you can enter the next stage, like any journey you undertake. So therefore, you need to re-ingest the knowledge that is waiting here for you before you can fully judge the validity of the journey you have just completed. There are similarities between your birth into the physical world and your rebirth into this world. You do not, however, have the need for the physical process that that world calls for but yet you do need to adapt back into this existence. In time you learn to leave that body you cling to behind. In time you relearn the senses you need on this plane. In time you learn to disassociate yourself with the concerns of earth life you have left and in time you learn to leave the living (earth living) to those on the earth. Yes, you may still be close to those you have left behind you but not in any way that will hinder your own progress.

Do not forget that the experiences that you gain in Spirit will also be relevant to those that will follow you and in this way your knowledge will be of great assistance to them. Remember the words quoted from Jesus as being relevant, "I go to prepare a place for you in my Father's house." So you see it is continuous progression, all the time helping one another to attain higher and higher vibrations.

Many words have been written trying to explain in physical terms the way it is here. All interpretations are valid insofar as they expand your thinking. Take these words and use them but do not be confined by them. There are so many dimensions in this existence that any perception has a certain truth. Realise that you yourself are your own limitation and when next you venture into this realm you can expect to access a different viewpoint even if it is on the same subject as before. Allow yourself this openness.

Go now with our wish for all God's blessings to be bestowed on you.

TRANCE.

In the infinity of timelessness and distantness, it is impossible for us to understand the confines of your space. It is therefore necessary that we undergo an experience in living in that space for a short while, so that we can better understand that which you have to contend with.

One condition that enables us to achieve that experience is whilst a physical being is in that state known as trance. We cannot over emphasise the degree of understanding that you must attain before this condition can be undertaken without risk to your very sanity. For you to volunteer to allow this condition to take place necessitates you volunteering your body for the occupancy by a discarnate being. If you do not have a clear understanding, purely seeking the phenomena, then you run this risk. There are those of this world that do not come from the Illumined One, and who seek such as you to provide them with the vehicle for travelling in your world, actively engaged in work of the darkest nature. We seek to advise you of this as there are many of you who seek this condition of trance, but not for the real reasons of truth.

We have spoken of the anti-Christ within every being, if this is what is manifest at the time of the request for trance, and by the law of like attracting like, then you will understand the folly. We need that you understand that trance is a tool of Spirit and as a tool does not confine itself to the use for the good only, but is a universal tool, good and bad.

Be not fooled by the trance phenomena for it is impressive. Whilst in trance there are many uses that the body may be used for. It may be used as a vehicle for a Spirit seeking body experience - as we have already discussed, or it may be used as a transmitter for messages from those in Spirit to those on the earth, by either using direct voice or by permitting it to be used for various forms of materialisation. Transfiguration is one such phenomena, and is no more, nor no less, an experience than any other.

Again, we stress that many who witness these phenomena do not fully realise what it is they are to experience. Many just see such as being a performance, which in itself it is, but this is not the real reason for their being allowed to witness. The reason should be a spiritual one and then you may benefit somewhat.

There is nothing special to these phenomena, other than the interest that they generate in relation to the self-searcher. It provides them with a focus outside of the earth plane and also allows them to perhaps enjoy a short sojourn with one who has departed that realm. Remember however, that though this is performed in trance, that the physical being is not totally vacated by the resident Spirit and that the life line connecting the two is very strong. Do not test its strength.

Our advice therefore is not for you to go seeking trance like states or indeed the facility of any other phenomena, rather let them seek you. In your time it will happen if it is necessary. You will have noticed we referred to Spirit that is not entirely wholesome, do not dwell on this, rather understand that there is an existence that lends itself to this description and see that it is not your existence.

To say that all comes from the One is not true for there are many givers. You can be a giver, your body is yours, you can give parts of it to others. Your body did not come from God, your Spirit does. So be aware of this and understand the flippancy of such a remark. You must define accurately where you wish for help to come from, before you seek it. We have spoken on this in relation to healing, now we speak of this again in relation to matters of further Spirit communication.

There are many who will answer your call for help. In calling for help in communication you announce your innocence to all and you may be assured that there are those who listen for such a call. Again, we stress that for you to improve your spirituality and grow more perfect, then it is only necessary that you address your request to God, and only to God, and sit in meditation to allow your Spirit friends to assist you in the transformation you have requested. Realise that though you request of your Spirit friends, they cannot act without the sanctioning of God that this request is to be answered. So ask God yourself, your Spirit friends will do what is necessary, all you have to do is wait.

Do not accept short cuts to this world, there are those who offer quick solutions to your requests for a spiritual way, remember that they have only their way and not yours. Proceed with caution where others of the earth are involved, seek your own truth always.

So to summarise the teaching of this time, we need you to help us understand the physical world, to understand your needs, to understand how we can best help you in the requests that you have addressed to the Light. You need us to help you expand your consciousness so that you can be more receptive to the knowledge that is given, to advise you of the pitfalls that you may encounter, and to bring you, through guidance, safely through the labyrinths into Spirit, and on to God. We have spoken of the Spirit world and of the death that allows your Spirit the freedom to enter it.

We have spoken on how you continue to live through eternity. We have spoken of the many ways that Spirit guidance can occur and how best you may be susceptible to it. We have spoken of the negativity that exists and how that can work against your evolvement, and we have spoken of the many human traits that can be overindulged in, also effecting the evolvement of the migrating Spirit. We have spoken of the multitude of ways that are there for you to tread, and of the many perils that exist along those ways. We have spoken of darkness but most of all we have spoken of Light. We have spoken of the many "gifts" available and of the plus and minus aspects of these. We have spoken of impostors and how you must overcome them. Most of all we have spoken at length of God and how He may be found within/without, and how He may be recognised.

Yes, this is a summary of these teachings and of all the previous teachings. We hope that you have received them as they were given, in Love and in Light, for these have been given to you in all humility, a humility that can only be experienced when in the presence of one who is so perfect, God.

Again and always we beseech Him to bless you in all the trials you have to endure in that existence, and that He will continue to allow us to be forever your guidance.

Made in the USA
Monee, IL
18 March 2021